Emile Zola

Thérèse Raquin

Claude Schumacher

Senior Lecturer,
Department of Theatre,
Film and Television Studies,
University of Glasgow.

University of Glasgow French and German Publications
1990

University of Glasgow French and German Publications

Series Editors: Mark G. Ward (German)
Geoff Woollen (French)

Consultant Editors : Colin Smethurst
Kenneth Varty

Modern Languages Building, University of Glasgow,
Glasgow G12 8QL, Scotland.

First published 1990

Printed by BPCC Wheatons Ltd., Exeter.

ISBN   0 85261 263 X

Contents

Preface

Page numbers given in the text refer to Henri Mitterand's edition of *Thérèse Raquin* (Paris: Garnier-Flammarion, nº 229, 1970). The essays 'Le Roman expérimental'—*RE*—and 'Le Naturalisme au théâtre'—*NT*—are cited according to the pagination of Aimé Guedj's edition of *Le Roman expérimental* (Paris: Garnier-Flammarion, nº 248, 1971).

An English translation of the play, by Pip Broughton, is now available (Bath: Absolute Press, 'Absolute Classics', 1989).

I should like to express my grateful thanks to my colleagues of the Department of Theatre Studies of the University of Glasgow: to Graham Barlow, for drawing the stage diagrams reproduced on pp. 70 and 71; to Jan MacDonald, for invaluable information; and to Brian Singleton, for his collaboration. Finally, *un grand merci* to Geoff Woollen for having offered me the opportunity to write this book, and for his supportiveness.

Glasgow, February 1990   Claude Schumacher

Introduction

Almost a century after his death, Zola is still the victim of ill-informed critical clichés which hinder a productive reading of his work. Too many critics have lazily repeated one another's accusations that he was both a boring 'naturalist' and a lurid 'pornographer'. The first substantial article devoted to *Thérèse Raquin* was entitled 'La Littérature putride' (*Le Figaro*, 23 Jan. 1868). In it Louis Ulbach, under the pseudonym of 'Ferragus', accused Zola of wallowing in the mud of the gutter, of exhibiting a lack of imagination ('ces imaginations malsaines étaient des imaginations pauvres et paresseuses') and of being monotonous ('la monotonie de l'ignoble est la pire des monotonies').

If the charge of pornography is simply ludicrous—and closely linked to the prudish and hypocritical society of the Second Empire—the theoretical question surrounding the problems of naturalism merits a rather substantial discussion at the beginning of our investigation of *Thérèse Raquin*.

The name of Zola is indissociably linked with naturalism, to the point where it would perhaps be critically more fruitful to coin the adjective 'Zolian' in order to evacuate from the critical discourse the ambiguities, misunderstandings and confusion which we shall try to dispel in the following pages.

Zola, of course, is the one who put the concept of naturalism on the critical map, presenting himself as the champion of the aesthetic avant-garde of the final years of the Second Empire and the first decades of the Third Republic (1860s-1880s). The problem with naturalism (Zolism), however, is that it presents us with two contradictory discourses, one theoretical and one practical, and—unfortunately—the two discourses do not correspond. It is also important to remember that *Thérèse Raquin* was published in 1867 and that Zola's main theoretical and polemical campaign in favour of naturalism dates from 1879-81 and culminates in the publication of *Le Roman expérimental* (1880), *Le Naturalisme au théâtre, Nos Auteurs dramatiques, Les Romanciers naturalistes* and *Documents littéraires* (all

1881), although the texts in which the word 'naturalist' occurs for the first time were written in 1866 (*Mes haines*), and contain already the essence of his naturalism and the seed of all future misunderstandings.

Zola multiplied the definitions of the concept, always insisting that the idea was both traditional (he counts Montaigne, La Fontaine, Diderot as well as Balzac and Flaubert among his direct forerunners) and eminently modern.

It has often been stated that the main inspiration for Zola's naturalism came from Taine and Claude Bernard (*Introduction à l'étude de la médecine expérimentale,* 1865), and it is a fact that he will endeavour to give his work in particular—and literature in general—a scientific dimension, the writer becoming a strict observer, experimenter and analyst, whose role is to consign in a report devoid of any flights of imagination the fruit of his exact and painstaking gathering of human data. We shall see that such claims are made in the preface to the second edition of *Thérèse Raquin.* In Bernard, however, Zola found only confirmation that what he was attempting to achieve in literature had a scientific basis (thus legitimizing and giving it greater respectability). But what he gained was offset by a far greater loss from which his reputation is still suffering, with the consequence that he is not yet read as widely as he should be and that his novels are approached from a defective critical angle.

Before coming to a few examples of definitions of naturalism, I should like to summarize a most important text written in 1864 to Antony Valabrègue (*Corr.,* 373-81). Zola is sending this long text to his friend in order to bring some order into his own ideas and he goes on to expound his theory of 'L'ECRAN' with the opening statement, oft repeated, that 'toute œuvre d'art est comme une fenêtre ouverte sur la création'. The artist must place himself in front of the world and depict what he sees, but even if the window is open, a screen, 'un écran', comes between the artefact and the world, since in a work of art the world is seen 'à travers un homme, à travers un tempérament, une personnalité'. Zola adds that 'la réalité exacte est donc impossible dans une œuvre d'art', since each artist distorts what he sees through the intervention of his personality. Having described the classical and romantic screens, both palpably false, the first for lacking life

2

and colour, the second for exaggerating colour and movement, Zola opts for 'l'écran réaliste', which by denying its own existence does not distort line or colour, but gives 'une reproduction exacte, franche et naïve'.

So far—almost—so good. Zola rejects the two main schools of French literature (classicism and romanticism), precisely because of their distinctive qualities, and opts for the most anodyne of solutions, 'l'Ecran réaliste, le dernier qui se soit produit dans l'art contemporain, une vitre unie, très transparente sans être très limpide, donnant des images aussi fidèles qu'un Ecran peut en donner'. If that was that, there would be no problem, no Zola, no *Thérèse Raquin*, and no need to go on.

But, immediately, Zola states that he cannot satisfy himself with a ready-made theory, that he has no wish to be a mere follower and, whatever the truth of the images created by the realist screen, they must be deformed and, thanks to that radical treatment, become works of art: 'j'affirme qu'il doit avoir en lui [l'Ecran réaliste] des propriétés particulières qui déforment les images, et qui, par conséquent, font de ces images des œuvres d'art.' He goes on: 'J'accepte d'ailleurs pleinement sa façon de procéder, qui est celle de se placer en toute franchise devant la nature, de la rendre dans son ensemble, sans exclusion aucune. L'œuvre d'art, ce me semble, doit embrasser l'horizon entier.' And he ends the theoretical section of the letter by repeating that what he requires, above all, is to feel the originality of the author in the work: 'me faire sentir un homme dans une image de la création'.

As Henri Mitterand rightly and succinctly writes: '*Nature, observation, document, enquête, réalité, analyse, logique, déterminisme*, tels sont les mots par lesquels Zola explicite le plus souvent le naturalisme' (*Zola et le naturalisme*, p. 26). Truth in literature as in science is arrived at after a rigorous and methodical investigation. Although the preparatory notes for *Thérèse Raquin* have not survived, we know that Zola researched most conscientiously the different societies in which he set his *Rougon-Macquart* novels: he went backstage for *Nana*, he visited the mines for *Germinal*, he studied Parisian slang for *L'Assommoir*, and so on. He also wrote to Valabrègue: 'Le mot *Art* n'est-il pas d'ailleurs opposé au mot *Nature* ?' In other words, isn't artistic investigation of a different order to scientific research and, here particularly, aren't the results of a novelist's investigation to be presented to the reading public in a manner radically different from the scientist's clinical formulation intended only to be scrutinized by his peers ? The question is silly and the answer obvious. But in his theoretical and political writings Zola often pretended that they were one and the same.

Zola was a man of deep convictions as his attitude during the Dreyfus affair amply testifies, and he was determined to change the mentality of his contemporaries in matters of taste, of morality, on political, social and philosophical outlook. He was equally adamant that his message should be heard and that he should be lavishly rewarded for his pains. When, in 1864, he publishes his first book, *Les Contes à Ninon,* he is not content to leave the distribution to his publishers. Although he judges his book to be 'détestable' and wishes that he could forget it, he has his own mailing list and writes his own blurbs for the literary pages of the newspapers: 'je travaille à obtenir pour mon volume le plus de publicité possible, et j'espère arriver à un splendide résultat. Dieu merci, tout est à peu près terminé'(to Valabrègue, *Corr.,* 384-5). Throughout his career Zola will devote much time and energy to the promotion of his work, sometimes stirring up controversy around his books, and, more especially, around the stage adaptations of his *Rougon-Macquart.* For a critic like Henri Guillemin, his various thundering pronouncements can and should be described as publicity-seeking propaganda. Such dismissal, however, would be as myopic as the vain effort of trying to read the novels in the light of the theory, leading to rejection of the artist because he does not follow the precepts of the theoretician.

*****

Zola was born in Paris in 1840, but spent his youth in Aix-en-Provence, where he befriended the young Paul Cézanne. In 1858, towards the end of his schooling, he returned to Paris with his mother (his father had died in 1847). In 1859, he failed his final exam (the *baccalauréat*) and gave up any idea of university studies. After two difficult years of poverty and casual work, he found a job as a packer with France's most important publishing house, Hachette. But in 1862 he got a transfer into the publicity department and soon he was running it. He used his position to become acquainted with the literary figures of the time and to find his way into the leading newspapers. From 1864 he wrote regularly in several papers (on literature, on painting, on current affairs, on artistic theory) and embarked on his own literary career. He published his first book, *Contes à Ninon,* in 1864. In 1865 he wrote a play, *Madeleine,* neither performed nor published during his lifetime, but which was to be rewritten as a novel under the title of *Madeleine Férat,* and published in 1868. Towards the end of 1866, *Le Figaro* published his short story, 'Un mariage d'amour', which can be considered as a first draft of *Thérèse Raquin.* 1867 was the year when his career took off in earnest. Not only was *Thérèse Raquin* serialized by the journal *L'Artiste* (August-October), thus bringing him a welcome income, but his lengthy novel *Les Mystères de Marseille,* which fictionalized a number of real court cases in the south of France, was not only published in a newspaper of that city, but also adapted for the stage (with the collaboration of his friend Marius Roux) and performed. The production was an abysmal failure, but Zola considered the experience worthwhile, as he informed Valabrègue: 'En ce moment, j'ai surtout besoin de deux choses, de publicité et d'argent.' *Les Mystères de Marseille* helped a little on both counts, and when, on 7 December 1867, *Thérèse Raquin* appeared in book form, Zola was well on his way to fame and fortune. Established writers like Flaubert and the Goncourt brothers publicly praised the novel, while Zola organized a controversy within the pages of the influential *Figaro:* Ulbach-Ferragus savaged the young author's work, thus ensuring maximum publicity and allowing Zola to reply just as vehemently in the preface added to the second edition. The preface is important on two counts: it affords us a deeper understanding of *Thérèse Raquin* itself, and it is a precious theoretical statement of 'Zolism' in 1868. But as the preface is strictly speaking a 'postface', we shall leave its discussion till later (Chapter Six).

A summary of *Thérèse Raquin* here is superfluous, since this study is intended for readers already familiar with Zola's novel. I shall also leave aside the question of sources or influences, which are of peripheral interest.

I shall try to signpost a few thematic readings through the book, in order to highlight the rich texture of the composition, Zola's use of intended or unintentional symbols, and to point to some of the many profoundly revealing echoes adding extra dimensions to the work. As well as being extremely satisfying such a multiple reading is also slightly disconcerting, as it displaces all received notions of a single-minded, programmatical 'naturalist' writer, and puts in its place the complex figure of an artist, meticulous down to the minutest details of composition, of a craftsman who ignores the precepts laid down by Zola-the-theorist, of a visionary who trusts the genius of his imagination above the logic of his intelligence.

It would be tempting to write from here on without any further reference to naturalism—or to the preface—and look at the work in isolation. Such an approach, however, would not fulfil the aim of this series, and I shall therefore regularly comment on the aptness, or otherwise, of certain features if considered in a strict 'naturalist' framework.

To end this introduction I should like to quote Henri Mitterand, the pre-eminent Zola specialist, who advocates such an approach in his preface to *Thérèse Raquin* (p. 32):

> Sous les thèmes et les agencements que manifeste la lecture linéaire, une relecture pratiquée en tous sens ferait ainsi émerger des structures profondes et une thématique seconde, qui forment, à l'écart des significations affirmées dans la Préface, un contenu implicite, un deuxième texte, dont le langage, déchiffré par les lecteurs modernes, est sans doute demeuré inconnu de l'auteur même, et de ses contemporains.

The pages that follow do not pretend to exhaust the meaning of that 'deuxième texte': they simply map out a few paths through it, for in any great novel there are as many 'deuxièmes textes' as there are attentive and sympathetic readers.

Chapter One

The Characters

'*Thérèse Raquin* est une étude de savant, l'anatomie exacte d'une maladie humaine particulière', wrote Zola a few months after the publication of the novel (*O.C.*, X, 757). In such a statement the author affirms, first, that his work is not a piece of fiction, since scientists deal with fact, and, second, that he is not interested in people as psychological entities, since he wants briefly to study a particular illness, from an anatomical point of view. In the notes he prepared for his series of twenty novels, *Les Rougon-Macquart,* we read: 'Mon étude est un simple coin d'analyse du monde tel qu'il est' (*R.-M.*, V, 1740). The analytical framework, provided by Hippolyte Taine, insisted on the importance of heredity, of biological determinism, historical contingencies and social conditioning (*race, milieu,* and *moment*), which clearly lay down that for each individual the die is cast at the time of his conception, and his future strictly predetermined. From Taine, Zola also took an approximate quotation as epigraph for *Thérèse Raquin,* which disappeared after the first edition of the work: 'le vice et la vertu, qui sont des produits comme le vitriol et le sucre.' The stress is on the material nature of all human manifestations. The psychological or spiritual dimension is not simply diminished: in theory at least, it is totally excluded.

If anybody read the preceding paragraph without knowing at least one novel by Zola, he would conclude that a novel by such an author could only be a dry and dreary piece of writing, about as exciting as reading a plodding police report. Of course, as we know, nothing is further from the truth.

Thérèse

Thérèse, the pivotal and eponymous character, is introduced into the Raquin family as a stranger: her mother was an Arab woman, possibly of high birth, 'une femme indigène d'une grande beauté' (72), who died when the baby was two years old. Her father, some kind of adventurer who will soon get killed in Africa, is old Madame Raquin's brother, and he took his daughter to her aunt as he was unable to care for her on his own.

Madame Raquin received the orphan with generosity, but denied her any individuality. The girl was strong and healthy but was forced to grow up 'couchée dans le même lit que Camille' (72), her sickly cousin who was anxiously nursed by his mother. Such unnatural upbringing is the direct cause of the tragedy that eventually overtakes her: 'Depuis l'âge de dix ans, cette femme était troublée par des désordres nerveux, dus en partie à la façon dont elle grandissait dans l'air tiède et nauséabond de la chambre où râlait le petit Camille' (184). Instead of being able to express her natural exuberance and passionate personality, she is forced to subdue her spontaneity. She lives withdrawn, silent, staring vacuously. Only occasionally does her vitality explode and then only fleetingly. This daughter of a beautiful Algerian woman and a French officer fades in the shade of the Raquin household, taking on yellowish colour and becoming almost ugly.

When Laurent first meets her, he sees in her the pale young woman that she has become: 'C'est qu'elle est laide, après tout, pensait-il. Elle a le nez long, la bouche grande. Je ne l'aime pas du tout, d'ailleurs' (89). Not knowing how to react to the new situation, as the only 'man' she has ever known is her cousin-husband, she resorts to her perennial attitude of passivity and indifference. But, now, her exterior behaviour hides an inner turmoil, too long contained, which Laurent senses ('Elle tremble, elle a une figure toute drôle, muette et passionnée' [89]). The stranger, instinctively, and because he opens his eyes, perceives that there is a hidden side to Thérèse's nature which Camille and his mother never suspected. Their blindness and egotistical self-centredness also carry a great responsibility for the tragic events.

Thérèse's first act of freedom, her first assertion of individuality in the face of the Raquin's constraining expectation of her is the adulterous act to which she consents. Despite its violence, Laurent's audacious initiative initially liberates Thérèse from the shackles of more than twenty years of imprisonment. And when Laurent discovers her in her bedroom at their first

8

assignation, he is amazed at her beauty: 'Laurent, étonné, trouva sa maîtresse belle. Il n'avait jamais vu cette femme' (93).

The beautiful, passionate, happy woman in love is a short-lived Thérèse: she is compelled to restrain herself because of Laurent's pusillanimity, and because of Zola's moralistic determination to paint a black picture of any sexual malpractice in general, and of feminine sexuality in particular. On the whole Zola denies Thérèse his sympathy throughout the novel, although a number of positive traits find their way into the writing. The little girl she once was smiled when she saw the retirement home on the river bank and her new, more congenial life, left her 'apaisée et silencieuse' (73). Also, Madame Raquin's decision to give her in marriage to her son is based on experience: she has witnessed the devotion with which Thérèse nurses Camille: 'sa nièce, avec ses airs tranquilles, ses dévouements muets, lui inspirait une confiance sans bornes. Elle l'avait vue à l'œuvre...'(73). In fact Thérèse checks her violent nature in order to please Madame Raquin, and uses all her self-control to present a face that is 'toujours doux et attentif'. After her meaningless marriage to her cousin and the heart-breaking move to Paris, Thérèse is so shocked by her new circumstances (which should last a lifetime) that she is totally numbed and unable even to express grief: 'Elle était comme glacée. [...] elle s'assit sur une malle, les mains roides, la gorge pleine de sanglots, ne pouvant pleurer' (77). It is difficult to reach further into the emptiness of despair, and impossible not to sympathize with a character in such a predicament. Thérèse endeavours to transform herself into an unfeeling, passive individual 'd'une complaisance et d'une abnégation suprêmes' (79).

Zola is at pains to avoid any reference to psychology, and insists on the physical description of Thérèse's behaviour, thereby eschewing the traditional analysis, which gives the author access to the innermost recesses of his characters. That attempt is both illusory and incomplete:

a)   Illusory because we read physical manifestation as the visible symptoms of some interior turmoil, of grief or happiness, and do not need the author's intervention to translate the flow of tears into tears of joy or sorrow. Quite simply, when Zola writes as succinctly as here, he puts us in the position of a spectator in the theatre who interprets what he sees without the need of further explanation or the need to read the stage directions.

b) Incomplete because, here and there, the all-knowing, judging author sneaks inside the skull of his character to reveal to the reader some insight which goes beyond objective observation. At the end of the preceding paragraph, I quoted from the text, but I did not quote the beginning of the sentence, which reads: 'toute sa volonté tendait à faire de son être un instrument passif...' (78). Thérèse's passivity is there for all, her mother-in-law, her husband and the customers, to see; but Zola assumes an authorial prerogative beyond the scientific remit when he informs us that Thérèse has to force herself to achieve that result. More blatantly, a few lines earlier, Zola peremptorily writes of Camille: 'Il ne pensait à rien.' Such notations enrich the fabric of the novel, expand our knowledge of the characters, allow us to approach these fictional creations in a way we can seldom be intimate with real people, but when Zola opens these 'forbidden vistas', he works as a creative writer, not as a scientist.

The beautiful mistress which Laurent discovers is the real Thérèse: Zola describes her as a woman radiating warmth, passion and an insatiable zest for life. She also acquires feline connotations of a positive nature, whereas in Vernon her animality was negatively presented. Now: 'La jeune femme, tordue et ondoyante, était belle d'une beauté étrange, toute d'emportement. On eût dit que [...] des flammes s'échappaient de sa chair' (93). Then: 'Quand elle était seule, dans l'herbe, au bord de l'eau, elle se couchait à plat ventre comme une bête, les yeux noirs et agrandis, le corps tordu, près de bondir' (73). François, the cat, who is killed by Laurent because he seems to personify the dead Camille, is at first directly linked to Thérèse's character. The comparison is explicitly expressed at the end of Chapter VII in a playful moment which follows the incident of the near-discovery of the lovers in bed by Madame Raquin. Thérèse imagines that the cat, always present during their encounters, could acquire the power of speech and reveal their secret. Carried away by her game, she becomes the cat: 'elle mimait le chat, elle allongeait les mains en façon de griffes, elle donnait à ses épaules des ondulations félines' (98). Far from joining the fun or enjoying the performance, Laurent is frightened out of his wits: he gets rid of François, and this seemingly trivial act looks forward to far more traumatic and violent events.

Zola continues the Thérèse-François comparison in his description of the young woman's attitude during the long, peaceful, friendly evenings around the dinner table which daily bring together the lovers, the husband and his mother. While the others exchange small talk, Thérèse remains withdrawn: 'Thérèse, immobile, paisible comme les autres, regardait ces joies bourgeoises, ces affaissements souriants. Et, au fond d'elle, il y avait des rires sauvages; tout son être raillait tandis que son visage gardait une rigidité froide'(101). The cat was just as deadpan during Thérèse's imitation of him: 'François, gardant une immobilité de pierre, la contemplait toujours; ses yeux seuls paraissaient vivants; et il y avait, dans les coins de sa gueule, deux plis profonds qui faisaient éclater de rire cette tête d'animal empaillé' (98). The woman and the cat share the same primeval instinct and savagery which will prove to be their downfall. A more erotic comparison between cat and woman explains why, despite his cowardice, Laurent cannot escape Thérèse's bewitchment. Her caresses are qualified as 'fauves' and this untranslatable term conjures up, in Zola's usage, extremes of sexual depravity, total lack of restraint and evokes strong sexual exhalations. Thérèse holds him under her spell: 'sa maîtresse, avec ses souplesses de chatte, ses flexibilités nerveuses, s'était poussée peu à peu dans chacune des fibres de son corps' (104).

Despite the central importance of sexuality in the novel, and of Zola's insistence on physiological explanations, the body in general and Thérèse's physical being in particular are curiously absent. In the opening chapter, Thérèse is discovered in profile, seated behind her counter and disappearing into the darkness of the shop. Zola specifically states: 'On ne voyait pas le corps, qui se perdait dans l'ombre' (67). When she receives her lover, she is in radiant white, 'en camisole, en jupon', but all Zola says about her is that she is skinny: 'son corps maigre' (93). Laurent, who after all is a painter and has seen many naked models, does not evoke the charms of his new mistress, quite the contrary. Afraid of Thérèse's passionate behaviour, when he had dreamt of a cheap and trouble-free liaison, he takes fright: 'Il voulait oublier, ne plus voir Thérèse dans sa nudité' (93).

Ironically when Zola writes that his heroine 'mettait à nu son être entier' (94), he means that she *analyses* with the sharpness of a consummate psychologist—who does not ignore the physiological dimensions of the problem—the reasons why she has become an adulterous wife and why

11

such an outcome was inevitable, given the circumstances of her birth, her childhood, her adolescence and, finally, her marriage. Zola makes her so articulate and so persuasive that, against the author's intentions, the reader cannot condemn Thérèse for betraying her husband, even if he stops short of condoning Camille's murder. Thérèse is aware of the burden of her heredity and complains that her upbringing ran contrary to her natural bent. Not only was the harmonious development of her body impaired ('J'étais accroupie devant le feu, regardant stupidement bouillir les tisanes, sentant mes membres se roidir' [94]), but her intelligence was also stultified: 'j'étais déjà abêtie, je savais à peine marcher, je tombais lorsque je courais' (95). Here one should perhaps point out a slight contradiction. Thérèse is evoking the time when the family was living in the country house, near the river. But in Chapter II, before Madame Raquin sold her business in Vernon, we read a feline description of little Thérèse: 'on sentait en elle des souplesses félines, des muscles courts et puissants, toute une énergie, toute une passion qui dormaient dans sa chair assoupie'(72). Zola further comments that the debilitating regimen did not succeed in weakening the strength of her body, and recounts how she once carried the fainting boy home. Is Zola, then, showing us that Thérèse is unable to tell the truth and lying to her lover even in the first heady moments of their affair? I don't think so, and would like to offer two explanations, refusing to choose between them (they are not mutually exclusive and could be accepted side by side).

First, Thérèse has such a negative perception of her life with the Raquins and such low self-esteem that even positive events take on negative connotations. It was Camille who could not run without falling, not Thérèse. *She* is the one who either picked him up or threw him to the ground in fits of temper (74).

The second explanation is that Zola-the-theorist intervened in the novelist's text. This is patent when he writes about a pre-pubescent girl that 'toute une passion dorm[ait] dans sa chair assoupie'. The notation is interesting in that it foreshadows future events but, strictly speaking, it is anachronistic.

Thérèse also reveals, in her conversation with Laurent, that she has been conducting a strict analysis of herself since childhood and that she is acutely aware of the dichotomy of her nature and of the tragic split in her personality: a docile, simple-minded, languid persona is opposed to a passionate, angry, revolted inner self appalled at her own hypocrisy and lies. A radical change, however, overcomes Thérèse with the start of the affair. She appears to lose her power of self-introspection and becomes a woman who wallows in wickedness and depravity. Unlike Laurent, she does not try to obliterate the memories of their love-making, rather deriving added enjoyment by evoking every detail in her mind while dining with the Raquins and pretending not to notice the presence of her lover:

> Cette comédie atroce, ces duperies de la vie, cette comparaison entre les baisers ardents du jour et l'indifférence jouée du soir, donnaient des ardeurs nouvelles au sang de la jeune femme. (101)

Having discovered sexual love and, for the first time, a *raison d'être*, Thérèse is devastated when Laurent fails to keep an assignation and then informs her that their meetings must cease. It is as if Thérèse were condemned to death at the moment of her birth. In a torrid but distressing meeting in Laurent's garret, the idea of Camille's death insinuates itself into her mind and together they half toy with the possibility of murder. The idea really takes hold of them when Michaud informs his fellow domino-players that many 'assassins échappent à la justice des hommes' (111). When the crime does take place, Thérèse's involvement is wholly passive: she is guilty for not having stopped it. Before the trip on the boat, Laurent already had the impulse of crushing Camille's head under his foot. Thérèse, seeing this, stifled a cry and turned away her head 'comme pour éviter les éclaboussures du sang' (116). Later she hesitates before entering the boat where her silly husband has already taken his place. 'Une lutte terrible se passait en elle', writes Zola, enigmatically. Is it a fight between right and wrong or between willpower and weakness? A combination of both, I guess. It is in fact the victim himself who resolves Thérèse's dilemma and seals his fate by his silly taunts: 'les ricanements de ce pauvre homme furent comme un coup de fouet qui la cingla et la poussa' (119). Thérèse does not help in the murder, nor does she attempt to save Camille. At the height of the struggle she bursts into convulsive sobs, and later becomes a malleable object in the hands of Laurent and the personnel at the inn.

13

A third Thérèse is revealed after Camille's death. Zola tells us not only that she has aged ('Elle était vieillie' [136]), but her body, which had been embellished through sexual fulfilment, now resembles that of a drowned woman: 'de larges plaques livides marbraient sa peau qui se plissait par endroits comme vide de chair' (136). Thematically, the image of the drowned Camille, which operates throughout the novel, is important here as it is elsewhere: the drowning of Camille tolls the knell of Thérèse's peace of mind, and of her sanity; it marks the end of all earthly happiness for her, Laurent and Madame Raquin. The descent into utter wretchedness for Thérèse, accompanied by her lover and her mother-in-law, is the harrowing subject of the second half of the novel. But, naturalistically speaking, the description is both a little premature and somewhat exaggerated. Thérèse's sudden flabbiness defies rational explanation: she is a young woman of twenty-five and almost exactly a year previously she was said to have had 'un corps maigre, presque vierge encore'(93). Again, in order not to resort to traditional psychological explanation, Zola oversteps the mark. Such a critique, justified as it is, would hardly spring to mind on a first or even second reading of the novel. Carried forward by the action and the ebb and flow of contrasting emotions, the reader of *Thérèse Raquin* is not troubled by such details. On the contrary, they add to the *effet de réel* pursued by Zola. This problem is akin for instance to the problematic question of time encountered by some critics of *Othello* who are worried by the material impossibility of Desdemona's infidelity. Given the tight succession of events in Shakespeare's tragedy, such critics are correct. But this 'structural defect' has never marred the pleasure of a spectator during a successful performance of the play. The same is true here even if it means that Zola puts a greater trust in his—and his readers'—imagination than in a strict, objective description of facts.

Far from being liberated by their crime, the two lovers become the prisoners of a situation they are unable to control, and Thérèse's personality evolves in many, contradictory ways. Her sexual hunger vanishes, she is even repulsed by a mere handshake with Laurent. Her mind *is* at rest, affirms Zola, adding 'Elle devenait certainement meilleure'(141). This particular authorial comment is puzzling. In what sense is she 'meilleure'? Zola seems to imply that she becomes more like 'everywoman', contented with her lot, 'curieuse et bavarde', and sleeping chastely alone in her 'virginal' bed. Thérèse acquires a kind of equilibrium which would bring the action of the novel to a standstill if a new element did not give it new impetus. Curiously, as much as from Laurent, that new injection comes from her newly-acquired taste for reading romantic trash. The books she reads give her a new 'sensibilité nerveuse qui la faisait rire ou pleurer sans motif' (142) and send her into extremes of apathy and feverishness. In fact Thérèse's sanity was compromised from the moment Laurent set foot in her shop, and a new life, which should have remained closed, opened up for her. The events leading up to the murder of her husband were all so traumatic that her feverish imagination could not cope. Her first horrifying nightmare occurs already in the inn where she is cared for while the search for her husband goes on. As we shall see in the thematic section entitled 'Remorse and le mariage protecteur', the infernal machine set into motion by the murder implacably destroys the lovers, but before bringing about their final destruction it rids Thérèse of any personality. She becomes the toy of circumstances, trying desperately and absurdly to make amends and, when that fails, to find escape into a life of vice. When both these routes are closed to her, and when the final illusory escape proves to be equally impossible, Thérèse submits and dies, committing suicide with Laurent.

Laurent

The character of Laurent is less problematical and more straightforward than Thérèse. Obviously Laurent is not introduced in the first narrative chapter, since his rôle as the outsider, the intruder, the catalyst, is to disrupt and destroy the peaceful initial image.

Laurent makes his entrance into the novel when the dreariness of the life of the Raquin family has been firmly established and when the reader is convinced that only something very dramatic can rescue Thérèse from her living death. The end of Chapter IV shows her slumped in a chair, holding the cat in her arms in order to avoid the sight of 'ces poupées de carton qui grimaçaient autour d'elle'(82). So far Thérèse has only come into direct contact with caricatural human beings. Then, one Thursday, Camille returns with a real man, and Thérèse cannot take her eyes off him: 'Elle n'avait jamais vu un homme'(84). At his first appearance Laurent is described from a dual point of view: his physical features are seen through Thérèse's amazed eyes, but it is the all-knowing novelist who fills in the details of his past which cannot be conveyed by dialogue. Zola also strays from a strict objective point of view in painting Laurent's psychological portrait in terms which clearly condemn the young man's life style.

Thérèse, quite simply, is lost in admiration at the sight of *the* male, the embodiment of maleness. Laurent is everything her husband is not. He is tall, strong, impressive, handsome. The luxuriant black hair framing his forehead, his round cheeks and his red lips all testify to his excellent physical health. Although the Raquins, too, come from Vernon, the confrontation is between the lively country lad and sickly townspeople. But what brings shudders to Thérèse's spine is the sheer sexual power which Laurent exudes and which, for the young woman, is concentrated in his thick neck: 'ce cou était large et court, gras et puissant' (84). She then notices that he holds his back hunched, and that he moves slowly and with precision, like a bull. Laurent also exudes a pungent animal smell which disturbs the young woman (87). The connotation is unmistakable: Thérèse, like Phaedra's mother Pasiphae, is unnaturally attracted to the beast and, should she succumb, a tragedy would inevitably ensue.

Zola, of course, is not entranced by Laurent and goes out of his way to blacken his character. First, in a short dialogue, Laurent tells Camille that he has broken all ties with his father because the old man refused to go on financing his loose living in Paris, where he was supposed to study law. When the pension stopped, Laurent turned to painting as an easy way to earn money. When this failed, he took up a civil service job that would not be too demanding. But his ultimate aim is to do nothing: 'Le père mourra bien un de ces jours; j'attends ça pour vivre sans rien faire'(85). The possibility, or even the probability of a murder is here inscribed. If Thérèse could resort to violence in a fit of passion, Laurent could well stoop to crime to satisfy his appetite. He has no ambition beyond the satisfaction of his various physical needs: 'Il aurait voulu bien manger, bien dormir, contenter largement ses passions, sans remuer de place, sans courir la mauvaise chance d'une fatigue quelconque'(85). In a word, states the narrator, he is a *paresseux*. Ironically, when Laurent eventually reaches a state of total laziness, the forced inaction becomes a torture: 'La paresse, cette existence de brute qu'il avait rêvée, était son châtiment' (239).

Zola deliberately constructs a contrasting, even a contradictory character for Laurent. Though physically powerful and fearless, he is a moral coward. With shameless vulgarity he boasts of cheap feminine conquests on first meeting his hosts. The idea of becoming the cuckoo in the nest comes to him in a flash, although he is presented as being usually slow-witted: in offering to paint Camille's portrait he is only making sure that he will be able to establish himself in the household as 'l'amant de la femme, l'ami du mari, l'enfant gâté de la mère' (99). To achieve this ambition, Laurent is determined to knock Camille senseless should he discover anything and object. Equally his 'seduction' of Thérèse is an act of violence, a rape. But morally the braggart is a coward. When he finds in Thérèse a passionate lover rather than the submissive sex object he was expecting, he takes fright: ' ...il la subissait. Il avait des heures d'effroi, des moments de prudence...' (94). Even the cat frightens him.

In the description of Laurent, the word 'brute' (e.g. 'tout semblait inconscient dans cette florissante nature de brute' [104]), occurs again and again. The 'brute humaine', or what Zola will later call '*la bête humaine* ', is characterized by a total absence of any moral conscience, and so it should be with Laurent. The animal imagery, if erotically convincing, does not, however, succeed in conveying the whole truth about 'human nature' in general, or a particular character, in this instance Laurent. Before the crime, Zola tells us that Laurent's body needs Thérèse as it needs food: today we might be shown a junky needing his fix or suffering withdrawal symptoms. Laurent 'se laissait conduire par les volontés de son organisme' (104). If that were all, there would be no story, because there would be no humanity. Unlike the rutting bull, whose instinct, in the wild, can only be checked by another bull, Laurent is aware of the constraints society puts on his action and, though dimly, knows the difference between right and wrong. His conscience manifests itself through fear, even if his stronger egotism makes him murder Camille. As for Thérèse, the second half of the novel plots the self-destructive path of a character whose immorality is not the absolute that his creator proclaims it to be.

Camille

The character of Camille, at first sight unidimensional, acquires its own complexity in the course of the novel. We shall see Camille as himself, as a creation of the other characters, as a portrait, as a ghostly and nightmarish apparition, and as an idealized image in Thérèse's deranged psyche.

The description of Camille given in the opening chapter requires no modification in the course of the novel. He is 'petit, chétif, d'allure languissante; [...] il ressemblait à un enfant malade et gâté' (68). A sickly child, Camille has only survived thanks to the devotion of his mother, but instead of being grateful for her sacrifice, the young boy expects his every whim to be satisfied. Not that he has any ambition at all. He is a kind of simpleton who hardly knows anything and who, at eighteen, is thrilled to get a boring office job. Although he knows that he is destined to marry his cousin, he never shows any sexual curiosity. Worse, when his mother mentions the subject of his marriage, he goes to sleep. A week after the wedding, Camille takes the only important decision in his life: he is determined to move to Paris. His mother is appalled at the prospect, but as he insists, she makes the journey to the capital to organize their new life: Camille himself does not lift a finger. His reason for leaving Vernon ? 'Il voulait être employé dans une grande administration [...] avec des manches de lustrine, la plume sur l'oreille'(75-6). His dream is fulfilled on becoming clerk 'dans l'administration du chemin de fer d'Orléans' (78), and he is so happy with his lot that he never misses a day's work. As far as he is concerned, life can go on without any alteration; he will be content to accept his mother's devotion, the silent presence of a dutiful wife and to work patiently for a far-off promotion.

Camille dead plays a far more important rôle in the novel than Camille alive, and Zola foreshadows his fate by scattering images of death throughout his text. The same paragraph which confirms Camille's self-satisfaction adumbrates that Thérèse, on going to bed each evening, is not so much getting into a bed as lying down in a winding-sheet alongside a corpse (79). More visually effective are her hallucinations during the never-ending games of dominoes which are the only weekly events that pull Camille out of his lethargy. Looking at the players, her husband among them, Thérèse is struck by the idea that she is walled up in a tomb 'en compagnie de cadavres mécaniques'(82). Twice during her love-making with Laurent, she speaks with disgust of her husband's sickly smell: 'je m'éloignais de lui, écœuré par l'odeur fade qui sortait de son corps' (94; see also 95). The same expression, 'odeur fade', recurs often in the description of the mortuary and the corpse, in contrast to the heady smells and perfumes of the lovers' bodies, from which they derive sexual arousal and satisfaction. To the olfactory theme Zola adds a tactile one, contrasting Laurent's strong body with Camille's corpse-like frailty: 'je sentais mes doigts s'enfoncer dans ses membres comme dans de l'argile'(95). All these images come together in the evocation of Thérèse having to enter her husband's damp and icy bed after having left the warmth of Laurent's garret. What she looks at with repugnance is the face of a drowned man, 'blafarde [...] la bouche ouverte' (109).

I shall deal separately with the portrait and the ghost, and briefly end this section by stressing an added ironic twist. As the lives of the murderers turn into an endless and unbearable nightmare, Thérèse—either because she wants to favour a forgotten past in the face of the ghastly present, or because her immediate aim is to torment her lover—sings the praises of her first husband whom, she says, she loves now even if she did not love him in his lifetime(231). The comparisons between the two husbands are, at that juncture, invariably favourable to Camille. So it is that in death the weakling acquires an ascendancy over the living which he never enjoyed in reality.

Madame Raquin

Madame Raquin is the fourth main character of the tragedy and the importance of her rôle grows during the action until she remains the only living presence left. She is an elderly, kind and generous woman who, during the entire novel, is presented as a static, physically immobile person. Of course her immobility increases as the action progresses, until she is indeed paralysed. She lives her life in blissful ignorance, devoting herself exclusively to the well-being of the son born to her in her thirties. Neither through reminiscences nor in his narrative does Zola mention the husband:

Camille is the only 'man' in Madame Raquin's life and she adores him.

Yet the very perfection of her abnegation is a powerful cause of the catastrophe of Camille's life. When chance gave her in Thérèse a second child with an iron constitution, she did not seize her luck and shake Camille out of the vicious circle of chronic ill health. Quite the opposite, she treated Thérèse as if she was sick too, and fed her Camille's medication in order to encourage the sulking boy to follow her example. She stifles the girl's vitality and stifles her *joie de vivre* in order to protect the boy. Her thoughtlessness is best illustrated by her attitude on her return from Paris, having bought the stock of the haberdasher's shop and signed the lease: 'Elle revint rayonnante à Vernon, elle dit qu'elle avait trouvé une perle, un trou délicieux' (76). The foolishly kind mother blinds herself to reality: her son wanting to move to Paris, she rushes there with but meagre capital, makes some unsatisfactory plans, and hopes that all will be wonderful. In the event, on arriving in Paris, she is slightly embarrassed, 'honteuse de ses rêves' (77). But she soon recovers her optimism, finds some advantage to compensate for each disadvantage, and her know-how soon turns the shop into a modest, yet going concern.

From the outset she treats Laurent like a second son, lavishing on him the same care as on Camille. In a sense Madame Raquin allows Laurent—*mutatis mutandis*—to 'broaden' Camille's horizons and to lift him out of his daily routine, as she should have taken advantage of Thérèse's sudden arrival in the household. In the stage version, Zola even states that Madame Raquin spoils Laurent by cooking his favourite dishes. It is she who has the idea of a small party, with two bottles of champagne, to mark the completion of the painting. In fact the expressions of generosity towards her two 'boys', then towards Laurent alone, are countless, until the fateful revelation that: 'Ce sont mes enfants qui ont tué mon enfant' (212).

She tends to ignore Thérèse as a person in her own right. She takes her daughter-in-law too much for granted. But she is capable of showing sollicitude even for her, and there is a kind of harsh irony when she tiptoes into the lovers' room, worried about Thérèse's health, only to be harshly mocked behind her retreating back (97).

The death of Camille is a cruel blow to her, and her fragile health deteriorates rapidly until she is struck down by total paralysis. But she behaves courageously. For the sake of her friends and children, she hides her grief and manages to be cheerful in her illness. This woman who enjoyed chatting with her customers is now sad to have lost the power of speech only because it deprives her of the satisfaction of being able to 'remercier ses amis qui l'aidaient à mourir en paix' (210). Only her eyes retain their expressiveness, becoming 'beaux d'une beauté céleste' and kinder day by day. The change that overtakes her at the revelation of the crime could not be more complete: 'Ses yeux, si doux d'ordinaire, étaient devenus noirs et durs, pareils à des morceaux de métal' (211). Her whole universe collapses, and she who had lived in the comforting thought that mankind was kind (the circumstances of Camille's death was proof of Laurent's and Thérèse's devotion to her son) is now convinced that 'tout est mensonge et que tout est crime' (211). The single thought that sustains her will to live is a thought of revenge. As her strength fails her when she tries to denounce the murderers, she resolves to starve to death, but resumes eating on realizing that, left alone, Thérèse and Laurent could possibly benefit from their crime.

Madame Raquin's character and situation undergo a total transformation. In Vernon she was mother hen, even in Paris it was she who organized the children's life. Her immobility, described in the opening chapter, is the expression of peace and contentment. At the conclusion of the novel, the active and happy Madame Raquin has become a vegetable, inside which there nevertheless has burned a flame of hatred sustained by the satisfaction of witnessing the self-destruction of evil.

Minor Characters

a)   The *jeudistes*

Some weeks after her installation in Paris, Madame Raquin, by chance, encounters an old acquaintance from Vernon. Soon Michaud, a retired police inspector, takes to visiting the Raquins every Thursday evening, accompanied by his son Olivier, also in the police, and his sickly daughter-in-law, Suzanne. The group is completed by Grivet, an elderly clerk holding a lowly promoted post in Camille's administration. Zola presents the foursome as a group of grotesques, only Suzanne playing occasionally an individual rôle. The four Thursday guests do not partake in the action, but Zola uses them as a prop to push the story along and to provide some much-needed comic relief. Their first indirect and comic intervention takes up most of the short Chapter X. As is his wont, Michaud is holding forth about his old profession, and on this particular occasion he affirms peremptorily that many an assassin gets away scot-free and that, unfortunately, the police are often powerless. Thérèse and Laurent listen intently and, at one point, 'leurs regards s'étaient rencontrés, noirs et ardents'(112). In the following chapter Camille is murdered. There is, obviously, no cause and effect link between the two episodes, but to hear confirmed by a policeman that retribution for a crime does not automatically follow strengthens Laurent in his determination.

Michaud's involvement in breaking the news of Camille's death does not shed much light on his character beyond the fact that his egotism is not in the least dented, but it reveals another aspect of Laurent's cowardice and callousness. While Madame Raquin is being informed of the 'accident', Laurent first loiters outside, on the pavement, 'il regardait les boutiques, sifflait entre ses dents, se retournait pour voir les femmes qui le coudoyaient' (124). Finally, feeling hungry, he goes into a pâtisserie and stuffs himself with gâteaux.The *jeudistes* are called upon in order to get things moving again, when the action is threatened by perpetual stasis following the murder. Coincidentally, all four decide on the same Thursday that the time has come to resume business as usual again (Chapter XV). Further use is made of Michaud to raise in Madame Raquin's mind the possibility of Thérèse's remarriage to Laurent. The presence of the *jeudistes* at the wedding helps to highlight the total divorce between the 'newly-weds' who start their descent into hell and the ineffectual and conventionally merry caricatures. Grivet's feeble attempt at heartiness ('Je bois aux enfants de monsieur et de madame' [171]) sends shivers down their spines. What in a normal wedding would be a happy toast reads, in this context, as a dire warning.

If, at the beginning of Chapter XXIV, the entrance of Michaud and Grivet can still raise a smile in the reader, a harsher brand of black comedy

22

is provided in Chapter XXVII, when the two fools continually interrupt Madame Raquin's desperate attempts at denouncing the murderers (216-7). Had she been allowed to spell out her message unhindered, she would have had more than enough energy to complete the sentence: 'Thérèse et Laurent ont ... tué Camille.' In fact, only three more letters (*tué*) were needed for the truth to be revealed. The BBC television adaptation carried the suspense even further by allowing Madame Raquin's strength to give out after 'Thérèse and Laurent ki...'; she then suffers the mortification of hearing this indulgently completed by 'kindness itself'! So having involuntarily confirmed the murderers in their resolve, the *jeudistes* now allow them to escape justice. But, as we know, their escape is illusory. The presence of the domino players on the night of the suicide further serves to underline the sadly ironic chasm between appearance and reality and the guests' blindness to their hosts' torments. Usually the three male guests speak in clichés, but on this occasion they outdo themselves and Grivet's final pronouncement before leaving is: 'Cette pièce est le Temple de la Paix' (251).

Suzanne is given a bit part of her own toward the end of the novel. In her despair, Thérèse invites this poor girl for whom she has only contempt to come and work in the shop in the afternoon. Instead of helping the ailing business, Suzanne's presence kills it off, since the two young women rudely despatch the rare customers in order not to be interrupted during their inane gossip. By lifting Suzanne out of her obscurity—from the shadow of her husband Olivier—Zola manages to sketch in a parallel between the two women, who become pregnant almost simultaneously. Whereas Thérèse brings about a miscarriage by cruelly taunting her husband, who does not need much provocation before resorting to violence, Suzanne is overwhelmed by joy and talks of nothing else during her last visit to her friend.

b)   François, the cat

If Zola often uses animal similes with respect to human beings, he also humanizes animals. In *Thérèse Raquin,* the cat has a very ordinary French name, but as the novel progresses François acquires an increasingly rich symbolic presence, without becoming simply the embodiment of one character or acquiring one obvious meaning.

In the introductory chapter François is nothing but a very ordinary tabby who does what cats do: he purrs, he follows his masters to bed, he curls up on a kitchen chair (68). His presence, so to speak, humanizes the Raquins' interior and adds a touch of warmth to a bleak description. He is still just a pet on his second appearance, as Thérèse strokes him on her lap to relieve her boredom during the game of dominoes; even more clearly than in the opening sequence, he is a living presence in the midst of the 'dead' surrounding the young woman. She looks at the cat 'pour ne pas voir les poupées de carton qui grimaçaient autour d'elle' (82).

We have already seen that Thérèse and the cat become very closely linked during the sexual encounters and, just before the rape, she assumes the passive, absent, rigid, enigmatic attitude often adopted by cats: 'La jeune femme était demeurée accroupie, regardant vaguement devant elle. Elle semblait attendre en frémissant' (91). Her stony exterior belies the interior turmoil, just as a cat's placid appearance can conceal a great deal of savagery. In passing, we should perhaps note that Thérèse herself compares her appearance, when Laurent first visits the Raquins, with that of an animal: 'Quand tu m'as vu, n'est-ce pas? j'avais l'air d'une bête'(95).

François's malefic presence asserts itself in the lovers' bedroom. He does not seem to approve of Thérèse's imitation of him, and when the young woman assumes sensuous, catlike poses, François, 'perdu dans une sorte d'extase diabolique' (98), retains a stony rigidity which so frightens Laurent that he chases the animal out of the room. From this point, the cat will never cease to haunt Laurent, who will kill the animal to free himself of his accusatory presence. Throughout the novel, Thérèse combines in her character the cat's sensuousness and his intriguing aloofness: Laurent thinks of her as a provocative sex-kitten at the height of his infatuation, and finds himself face to face with a surly woman after their meetings have to stop. Thérèse 'était plus immobile, plus impénétrable, plus paisible que jamais' (110). She has, to the ultimate degree, this ability so characteristic of cats not only to ignore the world but to make one feel that one has ceased to exist. These two qualities are brought into sharp contrast in the scene preceding the murder, and both act strongly on Laurent's resolve. During the stroll in the countryside, Thérèse quite unconsciously excites Laurent's desires by the cat-like movement of her hips as she walks in front of him: 'il regardait avec des yeux fauves les balancements de hanches de sa maîtresse' (114). The following moment, however, Thérèse is able to lie in the grass next to her husband and her lover and calmly close her eyes, pretending to be asleep. But when Laurent moves away, having in vain tried to arouse his mistress by kissing her leg, he notices that her eyes are open, although she maintains 'une rigidité froide' (115). She negates Laurent's very existence: 'Ses yeux fixes semblaient un abîme où l'on ne voyait que de la nuit. Elle ne bougea pas, elle ne tourna pas ses regards vers Laurent, debout derrière elle' (115-6).

The night after Laurent has in vain begged Thérèse to allow him back into her bedroom, some fifteen months after the murder, he lies in bed, unable to sleep, and imagines how he could rejoin his mistress. In his mind he sees clearly every detail of the way, every emotion which would stir him on approaching her. Because he is afraid of the shadows of the night, he does not put his plan into action, sinks into a tormented sleep and has the first of his nightmares: he returns to the shop, finds himself behind the bedroom door, and scratches. Instead of Thérèse it is Camille, the Camille of the mortuary, who stands in the doorway. This chilling scene prefigures the harrowing wedding night in which François plays an unhappy rôle. That long and unnatural night frays Laurent's nerves, but he manages to maintain a grip on himself until he hears a scratching noise. In their utter despair and dejection, the newly-weds imagine that Camille is visiting them and hide in the far corner of the room. Eventually they recognize François, who claws at the door to escape. Thérèse's earlier pranks come to Laurent's mind and and he now fears the cat's vengeance. He is convinced that Camille has taken possession of the cat and resolves to kill it, adding for himself: 'cette bête [...] a l'air d'une personne' (180). Although Thérèse prevents him from kicking the animal, Laurent is determined to rid himself of François by throwing him out of the window. For the present he lets the pet out in order to escape his accusatory 'yeux ronds, étrangement dilatés' (180).

Although not mentioned by name, François makes another brief appearance before his execution, in the shape of a drawing done in Laurent's frantic effort to produce portraits that do not resemble the dead Camille. Laurent fails in his attempt, since even 'les chiens et les chats ressemblaient vaguement à Camille' (205). Before plucking up courage to kill the cat Laurent plagues the animal, who stares continually at him and thus forces him to face his guilt. The death of François is also the symbolic murder of Madame Raquin. During the last days of his life, the cat seeks refuge on the paralytic's lap, and has now come to resemble Madame Raquin, so much so that Laurent 'se disait que le chat, ainsi que Madame Raquin, connaissait le crime et le dénoncerait, si jamais il parlait un jour' (240). Thrown against the black wall opposite, that same wall which so saddened Thérèse on her arrival in Paris, François agonizes the whole night long, to the despair of Madame Raquin, 'qui pleura François presque autant qu'elle avait pleuré Camille' (241), and causing Thérèse to suffer 'une atroce crise de nerfs' (241).

c) *La Marchande de bijoux faux*

Finally we encounter the most enigmatic character of the novel. Apart from the characters already mentioned, Zola briefly evokes, as the narrative requires, the Sunday trippers to Saint-Ouen, the boatmen, the innkeeper and the visitors to the mortuary. These episodes serve a specific purpose at a given moment of the story and fade away as the action moves on. Not so with the mysterious *marchande*. She appears in the expository chapter and on four occasions during the action. She never enters into contact with any of the protagonists of *Thérèse Raquin,* nor do they communicate with her. One is reminded of a similarly disturbing presence in *L'Assommoir:* an old, curtain-twitching lady is mentioned on three occasions, as she watches Coupeau working on a roof. Here, the idle curiosity is tinged with vicarious *Schadenfreude,* for when he falls off she appears 'comme satisfaite' (*R.-M.,* II, 480, 481, 483).

In the opening chapter the *marchande* is half asleep: she is a passive presence and mentioned, it would appear, simply because she is there and the narrator wants to fill in every detail of his description. Zola tells us that the passage du Pont-Neuf contains 'des boutiques'—shops—and along the wall opposite, a series of 'étroites armoires', very narrow stalls where the shopkeepers display some of their less valuable wares. But one of these stalls, precisely opposite Thérèse Raquin's shop, is the haunt of an old woman, apparently not a shopkeeper herself, who sells costume jewellery. Now that Thérèse is dead and the shop closed, the woman slumbers, but she is characterized by her alertness, or perceived alertness, in her other appearances.

Laurent notices her presence when he tries to sneak into the alley to meet Thérèse, and Zola notes that 'il lui fallut attendre qu'elle fût occupée' by a customer before daring to enter the house. Is the *marchande* really spying on what is going on, or is Laurent so guilt-ridden that he sees a spy in an indifferent old woman? Zola refuses to be explicit. But it is significant that one of the *marchande'* s appearances occurs not in reality, but in Laurent's daydream. Were he to carry out his wish, he would meet Thérèse at night and the *marchande* would not be at her post: '[il] se félicit[ait] de pouvoir monter chez Thérèse sans être vu de la marchande de bijoux faux' (149). Zola is at pains to inform us that Laurent and Thérèse lack a conscience, and yet he multiplies the tangible signs of his protagonists' guilt. The point is emphasized on the couple's return from their wedding. The *marchande,* faithful at her post, 'leva *curieusement* la tête, regardant les nouveaux mariés avec un sourire' (171; my emphasis). Not only is the character ambiguous, but so too is Zola's writing, or it appears to be even if the meaning was clear to the author. What does 'curieusement' mean? Simply 'avec curiosité', or, more likely, 'd'une étrange façon' ? This is, without doubt, the couple's interpretation: Thérèse and Laurent 'surprirent son regard, et en furent terrifiés' (171). The woman's gaze, as the cat's later that evening, activates their feeling of guilt.

Previously the *marchande* had briefly appeared after Camille's death. Zola shows her pointing out the young widow 'comme une curiosité intéressante et lamentable' (135). In this short passage Zola, intentionally or not, teases his reader: what is to prevent it being read ironically, the *marchande* being in fact far more explicit and circumstantial in her gossip than the text tells us?

Chapter Two

Themes

Camille: Portrait and Incubus

From the outset, Laurent considers the painting of Camille's portrait as a means to gain access to Madame Raquin's table and Thérèse's bed. There is not the slightest hint that it could be a generous gift or the result of a painterly inspiration. Laurent never had any vocation and took up painting because he thought it would be an easy way to earn money and to get to know beautiful loose women. Having abandoned painting to earn his living as a clerk, his only regret is the absence of nude models and the many opportunities for cheap sexual encounters. His paintings defy all criticism: they are 'boueuses, mal bâties, grimaçantes'(86). These 'qualities' exactly define the portrait, which is, if possible, an even worse piece of painting. Although Camille is a sickly man, he is still alive; yet Laurent gives him 'la face verdâtre d'un noyé' (90): not only is Laurent a tasteless dauber, but he lacks control over what he does. It is as if he is already painting the portrait of Camille lying on the mortuary slab; as if, subconsciously, he is wishing him dead before he seduces his wife. Zola himself, at this point in the novel, seems to have Camille's drowned face in his mind's eye, adding: 'le dessin grimaçant convulsionnait les traits, rendant ainsi la sinistre ressemblance plus frappante' (90-1).

To describe the corpse in the Morgue, Zola uses the same expressions as for the portrait: Camille is 'ignoble', he grimaces, his lips open in a 'ricanement atroce', the colours are 'sales', 'verdâtres', 'rouge sombre' and the body covered in 'taches immondes' (133). Ironically, Zola shows us Laurent lost in contemplation in front of the 'tableau qu'il avait sous les yeux' (133), but the murderer does not make the connection between the appearance of the decaying corpse and his handiwork of some months ago. 'Voilà ce que j'en ai fait. Il est ignoble' (134), he thinks regarding the dead

28

man, but the reader is reminded of the portrait too.

Camille's active afterlife, later to be powerfully linked with the painting, starts on the evening of his drowning. Left alone in a room in the inn of Saint-Ouen, Thérèse is victim of an hallucination, haunted by the figure of her husband, 'blafard, horrible, grandi' (125-6) fighting in the boat. Following the murder, the prudent lovers enjoy some fifteen months of relative peace, but Laurent's reawakened lust lets loose their suppressed obsession. He shatters the fragile equilibrium by voicing his sexual desire. Thérèse's refusal of an immediate encounter, linked to a promise to be his again when they are married, triggers off, in both of them, a violent nervous reaction. That night they are both visited by Camille's spectre. On his way home, Laurent, overcome by some irrational fear, searches his tiny room before going into bed. Unable to sleep, he imagines that his bed is rocking and that Camille is hidden under it. When, eventually, he falls half asleep, a nightmare takes hold of him: he runs to meet Thérèse but it is invariably the dead man who opens his arms to him. Thérèse is overcome by a similar obsessive dream, and in their separate rooms they spend an atrocious night of agonized sleeplessness which prefigures their dreadful wedding night. Never again, alone or together, will they be free of the avenging spectre.

The only fleeting moment of togetherness during the wedding night occurs when Laurent *sees* Camille staring at them from a dark corner between the fireplace and the wardrobe. Laurent is first unable to recognize his own painting which, in his terror, he cannot even remember. Eventually he sees his work for what it is: 'un tableau ignoble, mal bâti, boueux' and is struck by its unbearable ugliness and by its perfect likeness to the dead man. He is especially struck by the lifeless eyes, 'deux yeux blancs flottant dans les orbites molles et jaunâtres' (179). The murderers would dearly like to get rid of it there and then, but they are unable to take it down. In the morning, with the return of light, the banal and poorly-executed portrait loses its power, and Laurent can take it down with a shrug of the shoulders. The material object then disappears from the narrative, as such a support for the criminals' obsessions is no longer required. They have interiorized their guilt and will henceforth be haunted from within.

To escape from the infernal tête-à-tête with his accomplice, Laurent rents an attic to resume his activity as an artist. The chance visit of an art-loving friend affords the opportunity to inform us that his work has much improved and that his paintings are 'belles, [...] personnelles et vivantes' (203). But Laurent cannot find salvation or even solace in his newly-found talent. All his portraits, of men, women, children or animals, resemble Camille's grimacing features: 'elles paraissaient souffrantes et terrifiées, elles étaient comme écrasées sous le même sentiment d'horreur' (204). Realizing that he has lost control over his hand, Laurent destroys all his working sketches and gives up the dream of ever painting again.

Neither the hiding away of the portrait nor the fact that Laurent gives up painting lays Camille's ghost to rest. We have seen how Thérèse and Laurent were haunted, quite separately from one another, during the night following the discussion of their marriage. On the wedding night itself, Camille's ghost makes his appearance *before* the dramatic discovery of the portrait. Unable to behave as ordinary lovers when at last together in the bedroom, Thérèse and Laurent sit silently facing one another on either side of the fireplace. When they begin talking, freely for the first time since the night of the murder, they inevitably speak of Camille. Not only is the memory of the dead husband conjured up, but he appears 'in person' between his murderers: 'Le spectre de Camille évoqué venait de s'asseoir entre les nouveaux époux, en face du feu qui flambait' (174). Neither now nor later is it necessary for Thérèse or Laurent to communicate their obsession to one another. Each knows what the other thinks and feels, and each knows that, in front of the warm fire, the other experiences the same cold and damp presence of the drowned man. The constant, inescapable presence of Camille becomes even more oppressive and soon jeopardizes the couple's mental health. The ghostly visitor behaves more cockily with each succeeding night: he sits between them and warms his feet 'd'une façon lugubrement goguenarde' (185); he goes to bed with them, lying in the middle, so that if Laurent wants to caress Thérèse his hand encounters Camille's decaying flesh; he places himself between the lips of the murderers if they attempt a kiss.

Camille's posthumous presence in his home re-establishes itself more fully when Thérèse, overcome by remorse, fantasizes about the lost joys of her marriage to her first husband. It is as if the hallucination has become more real than reality: 'Le cadavre, qui hantait déjà la maison, y fut introduit ouvertement' (233). Zola introduces the unconscious and the irrational in his narrative to an extent which he declines to acknowledge in his preface, but his artistic intuition is certainly more reliable than his 'scientific' deductions. Laurent's essence, and to a lesser extent Thérèse's, is constituted by the act that makes of them unique individuals, and their subsequent actions destroy their very being. The uniqueness of Zola's work lies in the painstaking and meticulous charting of every downward step.

While Laurent is waiting for his marriage to take place, Zola notes that even more than the desire to have his mistress to himself, he was driven to kill 'par l'espérance de se mettre à la place de Camille' (158). The identification of the murderer with his victim does indeed take place, but not with the beneficial consequences he so blithely imagines. In fact, after the murder, he loses all the advantages which he enjoyed before Camille's death, and the contingent obstacles to his sexual satisfaction—which time and ingenuity could have removed—become absolute and insuperable. For, contrary to Zola's assertion, Laurent *is* tormented by conscience, and his possession by Camille starts on the day following the murder. The radiant young male who so overwhelmed Thérèse suddenly resembles his victim: 'le miroir verdâtre donnait à sa face une grimace atroce' (129). Why should that be? After all, we are told that he slept soundly, that he woke up fit as a fiddle, that he could hardly remember the previous day's event and that he was only moderately troubled by Camille's bite on his neck. Hence the answer to the question is buried in Laurent's subconscious, where we will also find the cause of the 'crispations' (129) troubling his sleep.

Physically the handsome Laurent degenerates and acquires characteristics associated with Camille, whose body was described as 'mou et affaissé' (86). Laurent now becomes 'mou, lâche, plus prudent que jamais' and seems to have 'ni os ni nerfs' (143). Like Thérèse later, he acquires the complexion of the drowned man, a 'visage marbré de taches livides' (185), and his trembling body experiences more torment than Camille ever did during his lifetime. He takes on the negative quality of being a model employee in a boring job, 'faisant sa besogne avec un abrutissement exemplaire' (143). In his hallucination, Laurent first sings Camille's praises (162), then gets the feeling of being robbed of his own identity since everything he touches in the house had belonged to Camille (233).

The final aspect of Camille's hold over Laurent proceeds both from an internal logic to the narrative and from the laws of human procreation as understood by some prominent biologists of the time. Between 1847 and 1850, Doctor Prosper Lucas published his *Traité philosophique et physiologique de l'hérédité naturelle,* in which he put forward the theory of impregnation. Put simply, the theory stated that a woman's children would inherit the genetic capital of her first sexual partner and not resemble their natural father if he were different from the first lover. The clearest example is found in Nana, Coupeau's daughter, who takes after Lantier, Gervaise's first lover. When Thérèse and Laurent blanch at Grivet's toasting their children (171), they are not conscious of any such theory, but when Thérèse discovers that she is pregnant, she cannot contemplate having his child. Not only is she afraid of giving birth to a drowned baby, but she has the impression of carrying in her womb 'le froid d'un cadavre dissous et amolli' (237). Thérèse decides to get rid of the foetus and chooses a very barbaric and cruel way to provoke a miscarriage: she taunts her husband and when he batters her, she presents her belly to his blows. So, unknowingly, Laurent kills his progeny. He has already committed artistic suicide; now he destroys any hope he ever could have had to live on in his children. The next step towards annihilation can only be his own self-slaughter.

The Eyes

In *Thérèse Raquin,* the eyes (*le regard*) play a crucial and very dramatic rôle, extending far beyond the mere act of 'seeing'. At present I have my eyes open to read and write, and a candid camera would not detect much in my stare: concentration perhaps. But if there were an unexpected knock on my door, I would look up and, according to who would step in, I would consider the visitor with joy or indifference, or... In other words, my eyes would start to 'speak' and, simultaneously, they would attempt to 'read' the message that the visitor's eyes would be sending out. It is also possible that little of this silent drama would happen because we rely almost exclusively on spoken communication and do not pay enough attention to body language. Lack of attention to the wealth of such information in Zola's prose would seriously impair the reception of his message.

Madame Raquin, following her stroke, lives on only through her eyes. She is otherwise totally paralysed and has lost the power of speech. But the eyes, or conversely the absence of eye contact, of the other characters are equally important. The theme is negatively introduced in the opening chapter. The narrator who, supposedly, sees things from afar and recounts events distant in time, first notices that the passers-by walk past the stalls without a glance and that the shopkeepers have a worried look when, 'par miracle' (66), someone stops in front of a shop. Reminiscing about the inhabitants of the haberdashery, the narrator sketches in the pale profile of a young woman, 'troué d'un œil noir largement ouvert' (67). The main feature of that elusive face does not seem to look at or see anything at all.

At night, when she goes to bed, Thérèse's vacuous eyes stare at the huge wall, again unseeing. In Vernon she forced herself to become a 'thing', a non-thinking object, staring at the fire for hours on end, 'les yeux ouverts et vides de regards' (72). In fact her clinical look pierces through the outer appearance of things, as when she mentally compares her husband's guests to corpses. The training she acquired while staring at nothing allows her to scrutinize Laurent without stepping outside her usual behaviour. The communication between her and her husband's friend flows through the eyes from their first encounter, and just before their first 'silent and brutal act', they stare fiercely at one another: 'Ils se contemplèrent pendant quelques secondes' (91). Such intense, not to say savage eye contact will occur again and again between the lovers (e.g. 107, 145-6, 165).

Thérèse only realizes the extent of her repulsion at Laurent's physical presence on her wedding night, but it is so deep-seated that no words are necessary. When he attempts to touch her she looks at him with 'un regard si étrange de répugnance et d'effroi, qu'il recula' (173). Earlier, while waiting for the wedding to be decided, they are not only afraid to be left alone, always making sure that a third party is present, but cannot bear to look at one another. But now, what they secretly feared does indeed happen. Their eyes 'speak' only about the murder and, looking at one another, they see the inescapable obsession which tortures their partner, thus increasing their own. For a time Madame Raquin helps them to overcome the worst: 'Ils n'osaient se regarder, ils regardaient Madame

Raquin' (196). But when they start suspecting one another or, worse, dreaming of a second murder, they are compelled to look at one another without respite: 'ils ne se quittaient pas des yeux' (248).

The cat and the seller of costume jewellery are essentially two pairs of eyes whose function is to force the adulterers, then murderers, to face their crimes. Staring at them, without a word (cats , in any case, do not speak), they signify that the outside world, although Camille and Madame Raquin are blind, is vigilant and that their goings-on have been noticed.

The case of Madame Raquin is particularly interesting. She is first presented as someone who is not observant at all, content to go through life without looking at the world. Camille was certainly a sickly baby, and his mother devoted to him. But she locked herself into that relationship to hide from the world, thus stunting the boy's growth and, by the same token, preventing Thérèse from having a normal childhood. In her blind devotion, she marries two children who are not suited to each other. We have already commented on the foolishness of the move to Paris. It only remains to stress Madame Raquin's total lack of intuition, either before or after her son's death. Never has she any inkling of the truth, and she falls easily for Thérèse's comedy of the 'veuve inconsolée' (158). Now, fearing for her niece's life, she takes a more active part in what happens around her and, with maternal solicitude, 'elle ne quitta plus sa nièce du regard' (158). Hence, a little before total paralysis sets in, the old lady's eyes start to open, but prior to that she is happy to look lovingly, 'avec des sourires maternels' (197), at Laurent. Once paralysed, Madame Raquin goes on living through her eyes, and the presence of her gaze for a time protects the murderers, as if she could still take part in their conversations. In the debacle of her life she is nonetheless happy, this revealed by two successive references to her eyes: 'Ses yeux prenaient chaque jour une douceur, une clarté plus pénétrantes' and 'Ses regards étaient beaux d'une beauté céleste' (210).

Then the thunderbolt strikes. Madame Raquin, at long last, understands the truth and the alteration in her eyes is immediate: 'Ses yeux, si doux d'ordinaire, étaient devenus noirs et durs, pareils à des morceaux de métal' (211). Henceforth her eyes become ever more expressive, more accusatory, more pugnacious, even if at times they also betray disgust and despair.

With consummate, but perhaps unconscious cruelty, Thérèse takes advantage of her aunt's paralysis to force her to listen to her confession and then pretends to read her pardon in Madame Raquin's eyes. Just as unwittingly cruel, Grivet prides himself on correctly interpreting every wish of his old friend simply by examining her gaze. Invariably he gets it wrong. Madame Raquin, for her part, has undertaken a struggle that must end with the death of her son's murderers, and her only weapons are her eyes. On the day she learns the truth, she has to be put to bed, carried by Laurent in the usual manner. She looks at him in utter horror ('elle [le] regarda avec des yeux agrandis par l'horreur'), and he mockingly whispers: 'Va, va, regarde-moi bien, [...] tes yeux ne me mangeront pas' (213).

Yet metaphorically Laurent *is* destroyed by Madame Raquin's eyes. On the final day it is as if she feels that the end is imminent. Having prayed to be allowed to 'repaître ses regards du spectacle des souffrances suprêmes qui briseraient Thérèse et Laurent'(251), she stares intently at them, denying the fussing Grivet the merest glance. After the guests' departure, the murderers—planning their new crime—avoid looking at each other, then sit down staring into space; when they turn to each other, it is because they sense danger. Yet before they die, 'ils échangèrent un dernier regard, un regard de remerciement' (253). While this final, silent tragedy unfolds, a lone spectator watches 'avec des yeux fixes et aigus' (252). And for twelve long hours, 'Madame Raquin, roide et muette, les contempla à ses pieds, ne pouvant se rassasier les yeux, les écrasant de regards lourds' (253).

'Les grandes joies et les grandes douleurs sont muettes', goes a popular saying. There are greater pains than joys in *Thérèse Raquin,* but very often words fail to express the extent of the distress experienced by the characters, or they are prevented by circumstances from expressing their feelings verbally. That is when the language of the eyes takes over. In putting such a continuous stress on silent communication between characters, Zola solicits the active participation of the readers in the creation of the fiction, for they must supply the withheld information either by filling in the missing dialogue (which is implied by the context) or by analysing for themselves the emotions conjured up by the text.

The Scar

'Elle arrêta un instant ses regards sur son cou; ce cou était large et court, gras et puissant' (84). Laurent's powerful neck operates unmistakably as a suggestive phallic symbol. A masculine body, especially in the 1860s, does not exude and cannot express sexuality in the raw as can its female equivalent. Zola chooses to concentrate his hero's sexual attractiveness in his neck, and it is precisely Laurent's neck which fascinates Camille's wife and provokes in her reactions she never experienced before (84). The phallic connotation, although repressed, is clearly evident in the chaste description of the lovers' love-making: 'La jeune femme s'arrêtait, essuyant ses lèvres humides sur le cou de Laurent' (95). At Saint-Ouen the sun bites into Laurent's neck and arouses his frustrated sexual desire.

Zola's meticulous preparatory notes, running into hundreds of neatly written pages per novel, have survived for most of his works; not, unfortunately, for *Thérèse Raquin*. It would be interesting to discover the various solutions which he considered for Camille's death, for he would appear to have hit upon the idea of the bite and the scar and then stage-managed the murder in order to achieve the desired result. The fight on the boat hardly makes sense, for the boat would turn over as soon as the two men stand up, or a push would be enough to send Camille overboard. It would be different if, for some reason, Laurent tried to remain dry, but as soon as Camille is in the water, he turns the boat over and jumps into the water with Thérèse. Why all these complications? Because it was essential that Laurent be bitten on the neck. In the stage version Laurent simply turns the boat over; there has been no struggle and remains no scar.

Thematically, dramatically and visually the symbol is rich in its ramifications. Laurent is wounded in his pride, which is his elemental virility. His neck, which acted as an instant turn-on, wil henceforth turn off Thérèse in disgust. The wound, a macabre love-bite, will ensure that Laurent will never be allowed to forget his crime, like a criminal branded with a scarlet letter. The morning after the murder, it is the burning sensation on his neck that brings back the memory of an action which he would rather forget. Placed as it is, the wound also keeps alive the thought of the ultimate punishment, since the death penalty in France was carried out on the guillotine (143). The sexual dimension is not forgotten: it becomes more harrowing as the novel progresses, and the image is sustained to the final episode. Angry at Thérèse, who has refused to sleep with him for fifteen months, the frustration causes his neck to have a surrogate erection: 'A cette pensée, le sang montait à son cou'(149). The sudden rush of blood causes a terrible burning sensation to the wound and his senseless scratching not only does not bring any relief, but the wretch has the feeling of being eaten alive from inside. The wound *is alive,* as Laurent discovers when he observes it in the mirror: when he feels an emotion that increases the flow of blood, the wound becomes 'vive et sanglante'(153), like some satanic stigmata. In his desperation he is, mistakenly, convinced that Thérèse will cure him with a few kisses, that his mistress's embrace will lay Camille's ghost to rest, erasing the physical as well as the moral scars.

Throughout the wedding day Laurent is haunted by his victim because his new clothes, bought with Madame Raquin's money, imprison him and because the stiff collar pricks his neck. During the religious ceremony he hallucinates, feels Camille's teeth on his neck and imagines that 'un filet de sang lui coulait sur la poitrine et allait tacher de rouge la blancheur de son gilet' (171). The image of blood is continued into the wedding-night scene. Looking at him as one would look in surprise at an intruder, Thérèse sees a 'visage sanglant' (174), and shudders. The sight of Laurent chills her blood even before he offers his neck to her kisses. The wound itself sends Thérèse into a frenzy of disgust and Laurent into a paroxysm of violence. She refuses to apply her lips to it until her lover employs brute force. Escaping from his clutches, 'elle s'essuya violemment la bouche, elle cracha dans le foyer' (178).

Later, when Thérèse makes a desperate attempt to banish her obsession by giving herself over to a frenzy of sexual activity, she attempts to cauterize the wound by putting her mouth on Laurent's 'cou gonflé et roidi' (190). She imagines that she could heal it, or at least get rid of Camille's presence, by imprinting her own teeth in her lover's flesh. For a time the rôles are reversed, Laurent having to defend himself against the vampirism of Thérèse. In the end the scar becomes the focal point of the couple's compulsive fighting, and Thérèse attempts to fend off the brutal attack by plunging her nails into the wound. As for Laurent, the tiny spot on his neck paralyses both his thoughts and his actions as he feels that 'les dents du noyé avaient enfoncé là une bête qui le dévorait' (239).

The wished-for kiss is finally given: Thérèse's mouth touches Laurent's neck as they fall, struck dead by the poison. This kiss, however, is presented as a violent action: 'la bouche de la jeune femme allait heurter...', and one filled with cruel irony: 'la cicatrice qu'avaient laissée les dents de Camille' (253). Thérèse's dying kiss joins together her two husbands.

Collusion

Despite Zola's repeated allegations to the contrary, and in spite of the narrator's many interventions to assert the primacy of the physical over the mental, the two main characters of *Thérèse Raquin* are both cerebral types, prone to introspection. After the startling coincidence which caused Thérèse and Laurent to suffer the same nightmare, which is to haunt them until their suicide and, indeed, drive them to it, the narrator notes:

> Cette communauté [de pensée], cette pénétration mutuelle est un fait de psychologie et de physiologie qui a souvent lieu chez les êtres que de grandes secousses heurtent violemment l'un à l'autre. (154)

There is no doubt that being linked together, first by an overwhelming sexual attraction and, second, by crime, the two lovers will share a community of thoughts and feelings. But it is questionable whether such a phenomenon is based on scientific observation and that it could become as systematic as Zola claims it to be. What is undeniable, however, is that his intuition regarding the deleterious consequences of a frightening feeling of guilt on a conscience generates a succession of subtle analyses, and that the intimate link forged between the obsessions of the two criminals increases the impact of their narration.

In Chapter XVI it is made clear that, had they so wished, Thérèse and Laurent were free to lead an unhindered love life. The reasons why they choose to stay away from each other will be discussed next. What interests us here is that they come to the same decision without ever discussing it. 'D'ailleurs, ils croyaient s'expliquer. chacun ce qui les tenait ainsi indifférents et effrayés en face l'un de l'autre' (141). Note the plurals *ils* and *les*. Zola does not describe, say, Thérèse's reaction, followed by a parallel with Laurent's, but stipulates emphatically that they both undergo a similar psychological torment, thinking the same thoughts, feeling the same feelings, sharing the same hopes and awful terrors. The principle established, individual reactions are noted, but even they proceed from a kind of shared feeling: Thérese thinks of Laurent only 'lorsqu'un cauchemar l'éveillait' (142) and he thinks of her as a dreadful nightmare. Despite their misgivings, their sexual desire for one another reawakens simultaneously, although Thérèse is determined to wait until her remarriage. When the nightly visits of the spectre begin, they have no need to communicate in order to understand what is going on: 'Ils devinèrent leurs communes terreurs car un même frisson nerveux courut sur leurs visages' (153).

On the morning of the wedding, they both wake up 'avec la même pensée de joie profonde' (168). This, unfortunately, is a very short-lived relief. All during the wedding day, they avoid looking at each other and exchange only trivia, but they share the profound conviction that they are now more distant from one another than they have ever been. The only feeling that brings them together is a feeling of terror at the sight of the *marchande de bijoux faux*. The scene that follows in the nuptial chamber is the most harrowing in a harrowing novel. Alone, the newly-weds begin a silent conversation which obsessively revolves around Camille: his murder, the appearance of the body at the Morgue, the question of his suffering. Even the occasional word uttered to break the spell is translated into an obsessive thought and understood to mean something totally different: 'Lorsque Laurent parlait des roses [...], Thérèse entendait parfaitement qu'il lui rappelait [...] la chute sourde de Camille' (175). They are intimately trapped in a tightening, infernal circle from which there is neither physical nor mental escape. Each knows exactly what the other is thinking and feeling, and yet they try desperately to keep quiet, convinced as they are that words would be even more devastating then silence. Vain hope, since they feel compelled to look at each other and since their eyes pursue an all too eloquent conversation: 'ils lisaient si nettement leurs pensées sur leurs visages, que ces pensées prenaient un son étrange, éclatant, qui secouait tout leur organisme' (176). Throughout the agonizing night they keep up these silent conversations, hardly punctuated by their sparse words, but interrupted by Laurent's attack on Thérèse, his hallucination over the portrait, and his irrational fear of the cat. After each incident the silence becomes more oppressive: 'Leurs longs silences les torturaient; ces silences étaient lourds de plaintes amères et désespérées, de reproches muets, qu'ils entendaient distinctement dans l'air tranquille' (181).

As Camille invades the bedroom space, the couple have no need to inform one another of the spectre's presence. Both are afflicted by the same fears, and both hope to alleviate their burden by putting up the same pretence. It is what Zola calls: 'l'hypocrisie maladroite de deux fous' (186). They feed on each other's fears and obsessions. In order to break the infernal tête-à-tête, they use Madame Raquin as a third party, and they go on using her even after she has learned the truth, but in vain. The cruel mutual interdependence which hastens the dénouement is only briefly interrupted by Thérèse's adulterous escapades. The end is near. Wanting rid of one another, they think of going to the police, but are unable to go through with it. So the final thought that occurs to them 'en même temps' is that of a second crime: 'tous deux sentirent la nécessité pressante d'une séparation, tous deux voulurent une séparation éternelle' (248). Laurent steals a phial of poison at more or less the time that Thérèse has a kitchen knife sharpened.

Not only do they schedule their attempts for the same day, the Thursday following the acquisition of the murder instruments, after the departure of the guests, but both telepathically choose the same moment: they try to act surreptitiously, but a 'sensation étrange qui prévient de l'approche d'un danger fit tourner la tête aux époux' (252). The time has long passed since they needed words to speak to one another. 'Sans parler', they conclude a peace of sorts and absolve one another before sharing the poison.

The intuitive mutual understanding of the murderers stands in stark contrast to the absolute blindness of the other characters, who never have the slightest inkling of the adulterous comedy played by the lovers under Camille's nose and, later, of the poignant drama that convulses the Raquin household. Madame Raquin herself, as her son before her, is not prone to introspection, and her lack of curiosity means that she is unable to understand the people around her and the motivation of their actions. Never in her whole life did she understand Thérèse, not as a child, nor as a young bride, nor as a murderess. She has a set of ready-made ideas that sustain her during a lifetime, and when events run contrary to these ideas she adopts another set of clichés, without any doubt ever entering her head. The same unidimensionality can be observed in all the other characters, and the contrast only serves to underline the rich complexity of Thérèse and Laurent.

Remorse and *le mariage protecteur*

Zola gives almost a neo-platonic dimension to Thérèse's et Laurent's 'union', noting that 'la nature et les circonstances semblaient avoir fait cette femme pour cet homme'(100), and he writes that together they represent 'un couple puissamment lié. Ils se complétaient, se protégeaient mutuellement' (101). The idea of 'mutual protection' is a theme that will be richly and ironically developed after the murder. If Zola shows us a Laurent moderately troubled as long as the corpse had not been found, he informs the reader that the murderer wallows in forgetfulness once the body is identified and the accidental death duly recorded: 'Laurent, tranquille désormais, se jeta avec volupté dans l'oubli de son crime' (134).

Although Zola is determined to concentrate on the physiological, he cannot ignore the psychological. Here and there the writer intervenes in the narrative with remarks to the effect that the subterranean movements taking place in the consciousness of his characters defy analysis: 'il se fit en eux un travail sourd qu'il faudrait analyser avec une délicatesse extrême' (140), and 'Il est difficile à l'analyse de pénétrer à de telles profondeurs'(203). Such disclaimers are both disingenuous and misleading. The novel charts in detail the 'sourd travail' that saps Laurent's and Thérèse's sanity, and the analysis could hardly be more meticulous. On the evening of the crime, Laurent falls heavily asleep, but his sleep is not untroubled: 'de légères crispations nerveuses couraient sur son visage'(128). Thérèse, for her part, suffers from 'brusques mouvements d'impatience' (135) against Suzanne, who kindly has offered to nurse Madame Raquin and the young widow.

When life resumes its seemingly untroubled course with the weekly domino games, Thérèse and Laurent appear calm and peaceful: 'A peine si parfois sa [Thérèse's] bouche, en se pinçant dans une contraction nerveuse, creusait deux plis profonds qui donnait à sa face une expression étrange de douleur et d'effroi' (140). 'A peine si parfois' marks the reticence of the author to acknowledge the insidious sapping process that is slowly destroying Thérèse. Zola states with firmer authority that their mutual sexual desires have gone, as if this was a simple matter of physiology. If, by chance, they brush against each other, they experience 'une sorte de malaise' (141), which they try to explain away as 'un reste d'effroi'. Had the sentence ended here, it would have been truer to Zola's stated programme, but he goes on to say that they also interpret their uneasiness 'comme une peur sourde du châtiment' (141). This is characteristic of what F.W.J. Hemmings calls the author's tendency to betray 'in all kinds of question-begging touches the moral assumptions on which his book is based' (*Emile Zola,* p. 35). In the weeks preceding their marriage, Laurent mentally rehearses all the advantages that his new position will bring him. But despite his forced optimism 'il éprouvait toujours, par moments, une anxiété qui étouffait la joie dans sa gorge' (158). Note the indecisive 'toujours, par moments', as if Zola were aware of a more profound contradiction but reluctant either to bring it into the open or to resolve it.

In their common torment and anxiety, Thérèse and Laurent also share a kind of forlorn hope that their marriage will prove a refuge into which they will be able to escape and protect one another from the torments of remorse. The theme of the protective marriage is introduced as Thérèse begins to suffer from nightmares which trouble her sleep. These nightmares, for which Zola adduces no reason and which he does not describe, bring Laurent to her mind, and she thinks that they would not occur 'si elle avait un homme couché à côté d'elle'(142). Her imagination conjures up the image of a guard dog, not of a lover, for she does not feel the merest 'frisson de désir' (142). As for Laurent, frightened to go back to his garret after Thérèse has rejected his advances, 'il pensait qu'il n'aurait pas eu peur avec elle' (147). This idea becomes obsessive the following morning, as the recurring nightmare has denied him any sleep (152). Yet each time they think of their marriage as a shield against their mental torment, they are overcome by 'un vague désespoir' (157), unable to ignore the impossibility of their situation. Zola stresses, in fact, their lucidity and their psychological acuteness: 'ils sentaient l'impérieuse nécessité de s'aveugler, de rêver un avenir de félicité amoureuses et de jouissances paisibles' (157). It is one thing to feel the necessity, it is another to be able to blind oneself to reality: Thérèse and Laurent fail to do so because they cannot lie to themselves.

Far from bringing them together, marriage drives them apart despite their expressed hope, on the morning of their wedding day, that they will now defend each other 'contre le noyé' (168). During the course of that fateful day, the comforting thought 'qu'ils n'auraient plus peur désormais' (170) abandons them gradually. That night, instead of starting on the road to recovery, they are brutally plunged into a nightmare more harrowing than what they have suffered hitherto, and the subsequent nights prove to be even worse than the first (182). The new couple do not succeed in abolishing the nightmares or in driving away the spectre of the first husband; their conjugal status is perpetual testimony to their crime, and ensures the presence of Camille, even in the marriage bed. Despairing coitus is neither an expression of love nor of sexual desire, but an attempt physically to get rid of Camille, and its failure starkly expressed in a one-line paragraph:

> Rejetés aux deux bords de la couche, brûlés et meurtris, ils se mirent à sangloter. (191)

Thus, while husband and wife measure the extent of their defeat, the corpse creeps back into bed and quietly lies down between them.

The only periods of relative calm enjoyed by Thérèse and Laurent happen when they are not together. They are so frightened to be left alone that they sit up with the invalid Madame Raquin every evening and welcome the previously despised Thursday guests. So adept are they at playing the perfect couple that they acquire the reputation of 'un mariage modèle', and seeing the dark shadows under their eyes, Michaud regularly remarks: 'Je parie qu'ils se dévorent de caresses, quand nous ne sommes plus là' (198).

The cliché 'se dévorer de caresses' brings to mind two further clichés which would be more apt, a fact of which the prurient old man is unaware. They are: 'être dévoré de remords' and 'se dévorer de coups'. 'Leur mariage était le châtiment fatal du meurtre' (219), and 'fatalement' the situation leads to violence: indeed, 'il leur prenait des envies de s'entre-dévorer' (219). Violence is already evoked during the wedding night. Unable to relate to one another, unable to speak, their nerves reach breaking point: 'ils pouvaient crier, se battre peut-être' (175). Their violent quarrels begin with low-key verbal exchanges, exacerbated as they are at being tied together forever. But verbal abuse soon gives way to physical violence: 'c'étaient des scènes atroces, des étouffements, des coups, des cris ignobles, des brutalités honteuses' (221). Their quarrels, which invariably 'se terminaient par des coups' (233), act as a perverted substitute for sexual relations. Not only do Thérèse and Laurent find some release for their pent-up emotions in these ugly fights, but Madame Raquin herself is stimulated by them: 'Une joie ardente luisait dans ses yeux, lorsque Laurent levait sa large main sur la tête de Thérèse' (225).

Sex and Sexuality

The question of sex and sexuality, particularly of female sexuality, is complex, complicated, contradictory, confusing, yet central to Zola's work and nowhere more so than in *Thérèse Raquin*. To do it justice a whole volume would hardly suffice.

The complexities and contradictions have their roots in Zola's own personality and are an expression of the double standards of male ideology in what we now would call a phallocratic society towards women. In letters to his friends, written in 1860-1861, the young man reveals abundantly his feelings on the subject of love and women. He clearly rejects the contemptuous attitudes which the young bourgeois, himself included, hold on the subject of women, but he is far from adopting a 'feminist' position. His own could perhaps be most accurately described as enlightened paternalism. Although he accepts that the institution of marriage as it existed then (and now) is not perfect, he can see no satisfactory alternative. Therefore he calls for a greater understanding and a deeper respect between the sexes. In his youthful enthusiasm he vows to reconcile 'l'homme et la femme', no less (*Corr.,* 129), and to take further the analyses conducted in *L'Amour* and *La Femme* by Michelet, whom he so admired. Marriage should only take place if it is 'basé sur une réciproque connaissance'(*Corr.,*

44

198) and should have nothing to do with financial or other venal considerations. Unfortunately the ideal marriage, if not out of reach, will prove to be very elusive because 'le bon ange', 'la rare exception' to the general rule of female depravity will be hard to find. Zola readily accepts that debauchery in women is caused by the lack of morality in men, which he stigmatizes harshly, but the feeling remains that, ultimately, women are to blame, for they should not yield.

The 'Pygmalian' ambition is a constant in Zola's thoughts. It could not be more clearly expressed than in his letter to Cézanne dated 16 April 1860, a fortnight after his twentieth birthday: 'dans toute femme, il y a l'étoffe d'une bonne épouse, c'est au mari à disposer de cette étoffe le mieux possible. Tel maître, tel valet; tel mari, telle épouse'(*Corr.*, 143). At the age of sixty-two, the author of *Vérité* (published posthumously in 1903) echoes precisely the young man: 'tout mari auquel on confie une jeune fille ignorante, n'est-il pas le maître de la refaire à sa volonté, à son image ? [...] Il est le dieu, il peut la recréer par la toute-puissance de l'amour'(*O.C.*, VIII, 1198). Almost half a century earlier, Zola had already bemoaned the young bride-to-be's ignorance. But then he rebelled against the thought, whereas the older man seems to accept the fact as immutable, and welcome its guarantee that the wife is the direct and personal creation of the husband.

Remains the thorny problem of physical sex. In his long letter of 24 June 1860 to Baille (which incorporates copied passages from a letter to Cézanne), Zola discourses upon love, the soul and the body, and concludes that mystical love without sexual involvement is as illusory as physical love without the communion of the souls: 'Qui écarte l'âme est une brute, qui écarte le corps est un exalté' (*Corr.*, 184-90). Had Zola, in his own life, achieved the wishes for harmony, we would have quite a different author to discuss. As Chantal Bertrand-Jennings writes, in Zola, 'l'approche de la sexualité est toujours une descente aux enfers, et la passion amoureuse toujours maudite' (*L'Eros et la femme chez Zola,* p. 127), this being so because woman is 'porteuse du double stigmate du sexe et de l'altérité'(*ibid.*). Both these concepts, of sex being a malediction visited upon *man* kind because of women, and of woman being the 'other', the *non* -male, are boldly expressed in another letter to Baille (17 March 1861, *Corr.,* 274-9). 'L'homme est seul, seul sur la terre', he resoundingly declares, in an absolute solitude specifically defined by the absence of communion with 'la femme'.

Bertrand-Jennings states unequivocally in the opening of her study that Zola's discourse expresses a 'vision catastrophique et infernale de la sexualité' (*Eros*, p. 11). In *Thérèse Raquin*, sexuality carries a negative connotation throughout: bad reasons bring about Thérèse's marriage, wicked reasons lead to her affair with Laurent, criminal reasons lead to Camille's murder. The one flash of light which suddenly pierces the gloom of despair occurs at the beginning of the illicit affair, as Thérèse is transformed by the discovery of sensual love. In her white camisole and petticoat, she overwhelms Laurent with her radiant beauty, with her tender and affectionate air, with the light that shines from *within*. The description of Thérèse in the first flush of love is indeed radiant, and the sour, sullen, soulless woman appears suddenly to have blossomed into a beautiful, if unexpected flower. The canker, however, is already destroying the beauty. The above description of the new Thérèse is not 'wrong', but selective, incomplete: I have left out the negative touches which, invariably, accompany the positive elements. Thérèse has not just a tender air, but 'un air *fou* et caressant'; she is not just beautiful, but also '*tordue* et ondoyante'(93; my emphasis). Her whiteness in her state of undress is contrasted with the 'sang africain qui brûlait ses veines' (93), and her clean, fresh smell with the 'air pénétrant et âcre' emanating from her body in heat.

Yes, Thérèse is not in love, she is in heat: when Zola writes that 'des flammes s'échappaient de sa chair' (93), he evokes the flames of hell and equates sexual obsession with demonic possession. Because Thérèse becomes an active partner in a shared love affair, instead of the passive and cold recipient of Camille's impotent and unwanted attentions, Zola calls her, in terms reminiscent of his repressed fascination, a prostitute: 'Au premier baiser elle se révéla courtisane' (93). She loses all control, her heart and her blood boil in her body, she trembles, she cries. In other words, she behaves hysterically, although Zola does not use the term in the novel. To confirm that in Thérèse there was vice waiting to manifest itself because of her mother's heredity, Zola drives her to prostitution and debauchery during the last weeks of her life.

Within the logic of the novel, one could understand Zola's relentless

46

indictment of Thérèse's depravity if her sexual excesses were contrasted with a former connubial harmony. Such harmony never existed and what sexual activity took place between Camille and his wife is never stated. One evening, 'Thérèse, au lieu d'entrer dans la chambre, qui était à gauche de l'escalier, entra dans celle de son cousin, qui était à droite' (74). And, after that first night, the young woman climbs 'chaque jour dans la même couche froide' (79), without any prospect other than the ultimate cold bed at the end of meaningless life. Laurent's appearance, one Thursday evening, has the devastating effect of a tornado tearing through an unprotected country. The French expression 'un coup de foudre' (tamely translated as 'love at first sight') is not strong enough to describe what happens. In front of Laurent, Thérèse is ill at ease ('la jeune femme éprouva une sorte de malaise'); while he holds forth, she listens, looking at him intently 'comme écrasée, ramassée sur elle-même' (87). On the subsequent visits of the 'painter', a force drags her to his side and she stares at him 'comme clouée' (89). She is still there when he puts the finishing touches to the portrait, 'accablée et anxieuse' (90). While Thérèse is suffering torments which she cannot quite explain to herself, Laurent observes her and coldly calculates his chances of success. Never does he become emotionally involved: he admits to himself that he does not love her but that his best interests would be served by an affair with her. Thérèse, in contrast, will tell Laurent that she loved him, 'le jour où Camille t'a poussé dans la boutique' (96). Yet, once more, that positive feeling is combined with its opposite, hatred: 'J'ignore comment je t'aimais; je te haïssais plutôt' (96). In her lover's arms, protesting her absolute love, Thérèse finds only negative values to express: she talks of her hatred, of her fear, her revolts, her shame, her weakness.

The various descriptions of love-making between Thérèse and Laurent do not contain an ounce of eroticism or the slightest titillation, and a reader picking up the book because of Zola's absurd reputation of a 'pornographic writer', so liberally conferred on him during his lifetime, would be sorely disappointed. In *Thérèse Raquin,* sex is so relentlessly portrayed as a harrowing and destructive activity that the book should be sold with a 'health warning': sex can be fun and healthy! Perhaps the most chilling moment is the initial sexual encounter: 'L'acte fut silencieux et brutal' (91). Laurent rapes Thérèse and the fact that she yields to his attack does not alter the nature of *his* impulse. Further encounters do not seem to humanize their relationship, for they behave towards one another with violence and brutality. Never once does Zola depict a quiet scene between the adulterers in which they flirt, joke or caress. The brutality of love is not confined to Laurent and Thérèse but seems to be universal, since the young women encountered at Saint-Ouen also carry the mark of sexual violence on their faces 'que des caresses brutales avaient martelés' (118); these 'fallen women' prefigure Thérèse's fate in days to come (see 244).

Following Camille's murder the theme of sex becomes inextricably linked with the idea of death. If, so far, sex was experienced as a dream turned sour, it will now overwhelm Thérèse and Laurent as an unbearable yet relentless nightmare from which there is no escape. Visiting the Morgue, Laurent is fascinated by the plump and white body of a young woman who hanged herself 'par désespoir d'amour' (131). He looks at her just as he considers Thérèse: both attracted and repulsed, he lusts after her and is afraid. He is frightened of the dead woman as he is frightened of Thérèse, because the idea of sex inevitably conjures up the idea of death. The corpse, half smiling and thrusting its breasts provocatively forward, is sexualized. An almost perfect replica of it is a picture that arouses his desire in the workshop of a painter friend, the model for 'une Bacchante nue, vautrée sur un lambeau d'étoffe' (144). The Morgue is implicitly likened to a brothel where men and women call in to indulge their sexual fantasies: a lady, elegantly dressed, silently stares at the body of a workman who fell off a scaffolding; young boys of twelve and thirteen joke at the sight of naked women: 'ils apprenaient le vice à l'école de la mort' (133).

For Thérèse and Laurent, the murder of Camille signals the end of all sexual desire. They killed in order to be free to enjoy one another's embraces without any restriction whatsoever, yet they choose to live apart, and they avoid one another's presence without feeling the necessity to discuss the new situation:

> Les deux amants ne cherchèrent plus à se voir en particulier. Jamais ils ne demandèrent un rendez-vous, jamais ils n'échangèrent furtivement un baiser. Le meurtre avait comme apaisé pour un moment les fièvres voluptueuses de leur chair; ils étaient parvenus à contenter, en tuant Camille, ces désirs fougueux et insatiables qu'ils n'avaient pu assouvir en se

> brisant dans les bras l'un de l'autre. Le crime leur semblait une
> jouissance aiguë qui les écœurait et les dégoûtait de leurs
> embrassements. (140-41)

Murder has satisfied in themselves a need which their frenzied love-making never did. Logically, Zola could end his experiment here, as his characters have found an equilibrium which will allow them to live out their lives. From a strictly naturalistic point of view, this is correct; but from Zola's artistic and dramatic perspective the action must develop towards a more compelling conclusion. Again the impulse comes from Laurent's sexual desire, whereas Thérèse seems now content with the monotony of life.

After their marriage, their sex life is a succession of acts of violence which provoke in them disgust and despair, acts that it would not be inappropriate to term rapes. The first occurs at the end of their long, agonizing wedding night when, out of exasperation, Laurent forces Thérèse's mouth on the scar left by Camille's bite (178; see *supra*, p. 37). The second connubial rape is also the last time that the murderers have sexual intercourse together. It happens a few days after their wedding, when Laurent is going insane with frustration, sleeping fully clothed next to his wife whose contact he must avoid for fear of further torture. So, one night, 'il prit brusquement Thérèse entre ses bras [...] au risque de passer sur le corps du noyé, et la tira à lui avec violence' (189). She responds to her husband, in the hope of being either destroyed or released by their coitus, and it is as though they are attempting to rape one another. At this point Zola's description is nothing if not fantasmagorical: we witness the cruel wrestling of two enemies trying to inflict wounds on one another, not in order to hurt but to find a release from their own unbearable tensions. The horror of the situation is, of course, heightened by the decaying presence of Camille, whose body is entangled in the lovers' limbs. The orgasm which they eventually reach is so painful and distressing that they start to sob, at either side of the bed, with the feeling that the laughing corpse 'se glissait de nouveau sous le drap avec des ricanements' (191).

For Zola, sex has only one justification: procreation. If the sexual act is accomplished by a virtuous woman in order to become pregnant, then such an act is good and sinless. Conversely, a sinful woman who indulges in forbidden sexual activity will not conceive, or if she conceives the result of the pregnancy will be more suffering (see *Eros,* pp. 92-101). As far as

Thérèse is concerned, the idea that she might become pregnant never enters her head until Grivet toasts her children at the wedding. She and Laurent turn white at the thought and feel cold inside: 'cette pensée les traversa comme un frisson glacé' (171). When, some five months after her marriage, she discovers that she is pregnant, having certainly conceived during her last, ugly intercourse with Laurent, Thérèse is devastated: 'La pensée d'avoir un enfant de Laurent lui paraissait monstrueuse' (237). Instead of a new life growing in her womb, she has the feeling that she is carrying a cold corpse and she is afraid that she might be giving birth to a drowned baby. As mentioned earlier (*supra,* p. 32), Zola accepted Dr Lucas's theory of impregnation, which stated that a woman's children would always inherit genetic characteristics of her first sexual partner, regardless of who the natural father is. Here, the foetus implanted in Thérèse by Laurent seems to behave as if it were Camille's offspring—and the offspring of the *drowned* Camille at that. So the dead man whom they tried to evict from their bed not only refuses to budge, but he has made love to his wife, just as in Laurent's worst nightmare.

After their unsuccessful attempts at resuming some sort of sex life, the situation between Thérèse and Laurent deteriorates very rapidly, and raw violence takes the place of brutal sex. Although the murderers refuse to acknowledge that their marriage is 'le châtiment fatal du meurtre' (219), they are unable to accept the constant presence of their accomplice. For Thérèse, the presence of Laurent signifies guilt and suffering, and vice versa. In that situation their hatred grows by the day: 'C'étaient des scènes atroces, des étouffements, des coups, des cris ignobles, des brutalités honteuses' (221). Their fights provide the ultimate release from the nervous tension that is accumulating in them day after day. Laurent finds 'quelque soulagement' in his wife-battering, but more perversely, Thérèse wallows in the pain as she would in sexual bliss: 'elle goûtait une volupté âcre à être frappée; elle s'abandonnait, elle s'offrait' (232).

The treble theme of sex, death and violence reaches a first climax when Thérèse taunts her husband in order to provoke his rage and 'comme il levait le pied contre elle, elle présenta le ventre. Elle se laissa frapper ainsi à en mourir. Le lendemain, elle faisait une fausse couche' (237). Although Thérèse appears to be a passive victim, it is she—in effect—who instigates

50

the attack in order to bring about her miscarriage: thus she becomes the active accomplice in another crime.

The second and final catastrophic climax needs no elaboration. Their obsession with sex has become an obsession with violence and death, which they plan to inflict on one another. The release which sex could no longer give them is reached in death, and the final tableau, eagerly contemplated by Madame Raquin, reunites all three protagonists, since Thérèse's lips come up against the scar left by Camille on Laurent's neck.

A rather derisory, yet somehow positive contrasting image to all this chaos is inscribed in the fabric of the novel in the pale character of Suzanne. Always in the shadow of Michaud and her husband Olivier, she acquires some individuality towards the end of the story. The lifeless young woman, described as a female Camille, seems curiously to soothe Thérèse's feverishness, and is invited by her to while away the afternoons in the shop. Yet it is this nonentity, this girl exuding 'une fade senteur de cimetière' (195), who represents normality and hope: pregnant, she talks ceaselessly 'de ses douleurs et de ses joies' (250). The counterpoint is by no means strongly marked, but it exists, and the affirmation of the virtues of motherhood will become stronger and stronger in Zola's work, while his condemnation of 'sex for sex's sake' will never diminish.

In conclusion one can only agree with Madame Bertrand-Jennings that sex, in most of Zola's œuvre, represents evil and that 'la femme est inévitablement liée au mal et à la mort, considérée comme le principe maléfique par excellence' (*Eros,* p. 127). Far from being a pornographer, Zola betrays the prejudices of a typical Victorian, and it was the hypocrisy and prurience of his contemporaries that prevented them from coming to terms with the reality depicted in the novel.

Chapter Three

Space

In this chapter we are specifically concerned with the various locations (loci) in which the action takes place. Zola, whose descriptions in the *Rougon-Macquart* acquire epic dimensions and become more and more lyrical and expansive (Les Halles in *Le Ventre de Paris,* the garden of Le Paradou in *La Faute de l'Abbé Mouret,* Paris itself in *Une page d'amour,* the plain of Montsou in *Germinal...*), creates in *Thérèse Raquin* a very claustrophobic, stifling and life-denying atmosphere, largely confining his action within enclosed spaces.

In a naturalistic novel in general, and more particularly in *the* novel which is reputed to have put naturalism on the literary map, one would expect to find a neutral and meticulous approach to the description of the environment. In fact, in *Thérèse Raquin,* far from being an objective background or, at best, a sociological milieu which helps to explain the characteristics of the main protagonists, the surroundings play a very active rôle in the fate of the characters. As Chantal Bertrand-Jennings writes in another important study:

> les lieux et l'espace ne sont pas pour Zola le simple décor d'une action. Ils y participent, au contraire, au point d'en être même parfois les générateurs. (*Espaces romanesques,* p. 32)

The first few lines of the novel are trivial enough and could *almost* be signed by an author of *le nouveau roman.* But the description is deceptive, and soon Zola injects subjective and emotive elements which affect the reader in an indirect way since he is conditioned to think that what he reads is a 'photographic description of reality'.

Thérèse Raquin is divided into thirty-two chapters. Twenty-one of these are entirely confined to Madame Raquin's 'boutique' or to Thérèse's chamber; a further nine chapters, including Chapter XI, the trip to Saint-

Ouen, either start or end up in the passage du Pont-Neuf. The two remaining chapters, which do not make reference to the boutique, are Chapter II, the flashback to Vernon, and Chapter XIII, Laurent's visits to the Morgue.

The geographical and 'moral' centre of the novel is Thérèse's bed. The bed could also have been studied in the thematic section: it is a recurring image here, as in many novels of the *Rougon-Macquart,* most significantly in *Nana,* where beds proliferate to the extent that they culminate in the erection of a baroque temple dedicated to vice, 'un lit comme il n'en existait pas, un trône, un autel, où Paris viendrait adorer sa [Nana's] nudité souveraine' (*R.-M.,* II, 1434). Now how, from a stylistic point of view, does the reader accede to Thérèse's bed? In the same way as one gets to the tiniest little figurine inside a nest of dolls, or in cinematic terms, at the end of an extended travelling shot. In the opening sentence Paris is silently evoked, the city itself never featuring in the novel. From the river Seine, the reader is led up a short street into a narrow arcade. Inside the arcade a shop, *Thérèse Raquin,* is indicated and after a short description of the exterior, we move inside the shop and accompany the three inhabitants up the staircase to their flat. Then the narrator invites us to follow the young couple into their bedroom, and eventually the lady is seen lying down next to her sickly husband. Aleready the dominant image is one of confinement, of suffocation in vaults, in tombs... The décor in which Thérèse is introduced is a landscape of decay and of death, from which there is no escape but in death itself. It is as if death, lurking in every nook and cranny in the passage du Pont-Neuf, is stalking its prey, and the monster will only be laid to rest when all the protagonists in the story are dead.

As in the case of the characters, a meticulous analysis of each cluster of spatial references would yield a wealth of information and deepen our understanding of the novel and of Zola's artistry. Lack of space forces me to make a drastic selection: I shall concentrate on the passage du Pont-Neuf, the bed and the Seine, but one could just as easily have chosen Laurent's attic, his workshop or the Morgue.

The Passage du Pont-Neuf

Unfortunately the Passage du Pont-Neuf has been knocked down to make way for the pleasant and airy space of the rue Jacques-Callot, so a modern reader has no opportunity to compare Zola's description with the place itself. But Saint-Beuve, whose criticism Zola requested, called the description 'fantastique' and stated that 'le passage est plat, banal, laid, surtout étroit'(49), in other words one of those nondescript places that exist throughout the world. How fantastic, then, is Zola's description? So fantastic that it is no exaggeration to say that every term of it is meant to convey an emotional message which must condition the reading of the subsequent pages of the novel.

The themes of death, decay and dereliction are powerfully stamped on the fabric of the narrative in the opening page. The first paragraph mentions the 'humidité âcre', sign of rot and deliquescence, which will characterize most locations. The passage is so dirty that even at the height of summer the sun does not shine through the glass skylight. Note the importance of the adjectives 'jaunâtres; blanchâtre; verdâtres' in the first three paragraphs, chosen in preference to *jaunes, blanche, verts* to denote the doubtful and dirty quality of these colours. 'Verdâtre', in effect, will acquire the status of a leitmotiv, always connoting death and decay. The reader is not so much led into a covered market as into an underground cemetery, with mausoleums along one of the walls belching forth their chilling draughts: 'des boutiques obscures, basses, écrasées, laissant échapper des souffles froids de caveau'(65). Opposite the shops, stacked against the wall, are narrow cupboards in which the shopkeepers wait for their customers. The image is one of coffins, an image made more potent by the knowledge that, in 1871, executed Communards were indeed exposed in vertical open coffins. Zola goes on to compare the passage to a 'véritable coupe-gorge' (the expression 'cut-throat' must be taken literally) and to a 'galerie souterraine vaguement éclairée par trois lampes funéraires' (66). This is where Madame Raquin chose to move from a country house near a river; this is where Thérèse is to be buried alive.

Inside Thérèse's shop, the merchandise is decaying, all the colours have turned 'gris sale' (67), and everything is damp. Upstairs the kitchen is black and uninviting. The couple's bedroom is bare and barren, and the window opens onto a high, black, badly roughcast wall which closes off the horizon, literally and figuratively. Thérèse will spend much time staring at the black wall, and in doing so she will reflect on the relative happiness she enjoyed in Vernon where she could at least look at sun-drenched lanes: 'Parfois, elle allait à la fenêtre, elle contemplait les maisons d'en face sur lesquelles le soleil jetait des nappes dorées' (72). Ironically the bedroom contains a second door: could it be an escape route? No, quite the contrary. It is an opening leading into the trap from which there is no escape: from the bedroom, out into the passage, back into the shop and so on. Let us not forget that the corridor is guarded, the old lady selling costume jewellery watches out of her cupboard, and to be trapped here is a fate no more enviable than to be lost in *Phèdre'*s Minoan labyrinth. Zola was fascinated by Racine's tragedy, and the fate of Phèdre is not irrelevant in our reading of Thérèse's destiny: a similar sexual curse destroys them both. Zola was soon to write a fuller version of the myth, transposed into the salons of the Second Empire. Renée Saccard, the heroine of *La Curée,* is driven to incest, then struck dead in her prime by meningitis. On the prompting of Sarah Bernhardt, the renowned interpreter of Phèdre, Zola adapted this novel for the stage, under the title of *Renée,* but the actress was frightened by the immediacy that the contemporary setting lent to the ancient tale, and declined to perform the modern tragedy.

The contrast with Vernon is less complete than it would at first appear, since even there, despite the presence of two children, Madame Raquin led the life of a recluse in a house always closed, always silent, and resembling a cloister. However, the open air was not too remote, and Thérèse had the odd happy moment when she could play, like a child, on the river bank. Her arrival in Paris is, for her, a descent into the nether world. Her aunt had promised that she had found 'un trou délicieux, en plein Paris' (76), but hardly: the imagery of the graveyard is instantly reactivated: 'il lui sembla qu'elle descendait dans la terre grasse d'une fosse. [...] Elle était comme glacée' (77). Life is so utterly drained out of her that she is unable to cry at the prospect of having to spend the rest of her life in such a godforsaken place. Before Laurent's arrival, Thérèse steadfastly refuses to decorate the flat, which provokes in her harrowing hallucinations, especially on the occasion of the Thursday meetings: 'elle se croyait enfouie au fond d'une caverne, en compagnie de cadavres mécaniques' (82). Laurent himself, despite the dinginess of his own garret (it belongs to the same world and is described with the same vocabulary), is struck by the humidity and the bleakness of Thérèse's surroundings, and he thinks to himself:'Une femme doit mourir là-dedans' (89). Camille's portrait, too, pertains to that decaying milieu which directly influences the painter's style.

Hoping that Laurent's love will help her escape to a new life, Thérèse articulates aloud the oppression she has felt since her arrival in Paris: 'on m'a enterrée toute vive dans cette ignoble boutique' (95). Little does she know that her happiness will be short-lived, and soon the great black wall will help to calm her anxieties following Camille's murder (142). Now that Madame Raquin no longer has her son to fuss over, even she realizes how life-denying her surroundings are, and she too thinks of the 'boutique' as a 'tombeau' (160). In effect the old lady is to suffer a fate worse than death. Thérèse's recurrent hallucinations of being buried alive (see 195) are becoming a reality for the paralysed woman. Not only is she a 'cadavre vivant à moitié' (206) for Thérèse and Laurent, but she herself experiences the torment of one buried alive—although by a writer's coquetry Zola pretends not to be sure of what goes on in her mind: 'Son esprit était comme un de ces vivants qu'on ensevelit par mégarde et qui se réveillent dans la nuit de la terre' (209 and, again, 211).

As Laurent and Thérèse move inexorably towards further turpitude and crime, their flat turns into a disgusting pit of dirt and humidity. They are trapped in the middle of this labyrinth as surely as the victims of the Minotaur and as permanently as a corpse in a grave: 'Ils étaient de nouveau dans le logement sombre et humide du passage, ils y étaient comme emprisonnés désormais' (247). The final image concretizes the opening, ghoulish description of the passage. The inhabitants of its innermost recesses have been ensnared by the destructive force which was lurking there, and they have been driven to self-destruction as much by the unwholesome surroundings of the passage du Pont-Neuf as by 'les fatalités de leur chair' (60).

The Bed

The 'act of the flesh' is traditionally consummated, in life and in fiction, on a bed, and the word itself carries with it a host of sexual connotations. It is therefore no surprise that the bed plays a central rôle in the geography of *Thérèse Raquin*. But the novel being a study of the sexual behaviour of two 'brutes humaines', the absence of the bed at crucial moments is as significant as its presence in other circumstances. As one would expect, the bed is first mentioned when Laurent makes his entrance. In his very first conversation he boasts about his feminine successes, and Zola writes that 'il rêvait une vie de voluptés à bon marché, une belle vie pleine de femmes, de repos sur des divans' (85). The reference to 'divans' at once introduces the note of seediness which is associated with Laurent's sexual activities. His seduction of Thérèse comes about because of his animal presence, which is a powerful contrast to Camille's deliquescence and is finally sealed by a rape. A rape—by its very nature—is a crime that does not require the complicity of a bed for its perpetration, and so it happens that Thérèse's fall into adultery takes place on the floor of the dining-room.

The adulterous bed, as the repository of love, features only very fleetingly and it is fitting that on the last occasion that Laurent is shown visiting his mistress, he must hide under the covers and on the floor: Madame Raquin is chasing him out and comes between them, as Camille's ghost will later drive the lovers apart.

After the murder the bed becomes 'un lieu maudit' for all three survivors, Madame Raquin included, although for a time Thérèse finds solace in the fact that she is, again, sleeping alone as when she was a child: 'La nuit, seule dans son lit, elle se trouvait heureuse [...]. Elle se croyait petite fille, vierge' (141). But such peace of mind is a delusion, since like a shabby latter-day Macbeth, Laurent 'hath murthered sleep'. The night following Camille's death, Madame Raquin suffers from 'un violent délire', Thérèse falls down from nervous exhaustion and Laurent's face is disturbed by 'légères crispations nerveuses' (128). This is only the beginning of their mental torments. The more spectacular manifestations of the effects the crime had on its authors happens, first, in and around Laurent's bed, then in and around the couple's bed. Laurent's hallucinations start one night when, for no specific reason, he is afraid to return home. He sees frightening shadows on the walls of his corridor and, once in his room, he locks the door and looks under the bed to check if no one is hidden there. Satisfied that he is alone, and smiling at his own cowardice, he goes to bed, but instead of going calmly to sleep he has the first of a series of nightmares, culminating in the sensation that the bed is being violently shaken by Camille: 'Hagard, les cheveux dressés sur la tête, il se cramponna à son matelas, croyant que les secousses devenaient de plus en plus violentes' (150). This scene foreshadows the ghastly episode which I have called the third rape. The furious love-making in which 'love' plays no part, the carnal battle that ensues, obviously causes the bed to rock, but in their hallucinatory state, the wretches believe that Camille is stalking them: 'ils s'imaginaient que le noyé les tirait par les pieds et imprimait au lit de violentes secousses' (190). In passing, one could also mention that the French expression (and superstition) 'tirer par les pieds' means that dead people, and especially those who were victims of ill treatment, will return and pull the living into the grave by their feet.

'La couche conjugale', Thérèse's and Laurent's connubial bed, belongs equally to Camille, and it is from their failure to get rid of the corpse that stems their defeat. The bed, focal point of the bedchamber, should obliterate all surroundings on a wedding night. But the newly-weds are afraid even to look at it. They sit and talk, facing the fireplace, and when Laurent starts a movement toward the bed he does not complete it, but turns violently to Thérèse in an aggressive gesture that leads to the young woman's second rape (177-8). For reasons that have nothing in common with the initial attack, the encounter again does not take place on the bed.

The last reference to the bed introduces the climactic episode in the novel:

> —Eh bien ! nous ne nous couchons pas ? demanda Laurent qui semblait sortir en sursaut d'un rêve.
> —Si, si, nous nous couchons, répondit Thérèse en frissonnant, comme si elle avait eu grand froid. (252)

Neither is thinking of going to bed, neither is inviting the other to follow him or her to bed—both are preparing the death of their partner and the invitation is an invitation to the grave and the ultimate sleep. As they fall to the ground, killed by Laurent's poison, they are for the last time denied the consolation that the deathbed might have given them. They lie there, on the hard surface, just as Camille was stretched out on the slab of the Morgue. And as Laurent stared at the corpse of his victim, so Madame Raquin stares at her son's murderers.

La Seine

The other spaces evoked in the novel equally operate on several levels and are never presented as neutral topographical locations. A typical example is the countryside at Saint-Ouen, scene of Camille's murder, where nature acts as a powerful accomplice. The murder is staged at the beginning of autumn at a time when 'des souffles froids commençaient, le soir, à faire frissonner l'air' (114). At Saint-Ouen, then a favourite Sunday outing spot for Parisians, an ordinary 'bouquet d'arbres' takes on, in Zola's text, the appearance of a huge, menacing forest that engulfs Thérèse, Laurent and Camille in an atmosphere of death foreboding murder: 'Ils étaient au désert, dans un trou mélancolique, dans une étroite clairière silencieuse et fraîche' (114-5). To heighten the ominous tension of the moment, Zola notes: 'Tout autour d'eux, ils entendaient la Seine gronder' (115). The river Seine, especially as it leaves Paris, is no roaring torrent but a placid waterway. The roar, then, is the roar that rages in the head of the frustrated lovers, but projected onto the surrounding nature. The powerful autumnal smells ('les senteurs âpres de la terre') equally stir Laurent's senses and are responsible for the murderous thoughts germinating in his mind, and the plan of the murder is directly inspired by the river, which he contemplates 'd'un air stupide' (116). But if, on the one hand, nature incites Laurent to accomplish the deed, on the other it remains aloof and indifferent as the sun disappears over the horizon and abandons the humans to their meaningless agitation.

Just before the description of the murder, Zola's prose scales the heights of romanticism: nature in its totality is in turmoil and tortured by tragic expectation. The autumn leaves no longer 'fall', they are thrown away by the trees ('les arbres vieillis jettent leurs feuilles'); the approach of death is consciously experienced by the countryside and in the sky one hears 'des souffles plaintifs de désespérance'. Zola even has recourse to the clichéd night = shroud comparison, but in this instance the image is to be taken literally: a shroud will soon be required. To increase the dramatic impact and to add urgency to the description, Zola (and this is a major stylistic departure in the novel) suddenly uses the present tense. Far from giving us a documentary account, or a clinical police report on the circumstances of a crime, he creates suspense and atmosphere in the manner of film makers like Hitchcock or Lang.

The Seine features several times in the narrative, and every description of the river reflects the state of mind of the character associated with it. Here are a few of the more telling examples:

p. 73 — young Thérèse, in a defiant mood, looks at the river which roars ('grondait') and threatens to engulf her;

p. 78 — Camille vacuously stares at the water; the river passively carries along timber rafts;

p. 89 — before his affair starts, Laurent daydreams, staring at the river; the presence of the Seine is almost irrelevant:

pp. 115-22 — the murder (see above);

p. 156 — the Seine is part of Laurent's nightmarish landscape and the innocuous tree-trunks which Camille gaped at (78) are now replaced by bodies in the murderer's feverish imagination;

p. 193 — but when, at the beginning of his marriage, Laurent finds some peace of mind outside the passage, the river welcomes him 'avec des bruits caressants'.

*****

It is not enough to say that Zola makes a subjective use of the external world: his description of the world is often presented through the subjectivity of his own characters. The point of view changes, the perception of the world alters according to the changing circumstances or moods of the characters and, thus, the geography in *Thérèse Raquin* plays a part that is as active and significant as that of any of its protagonists.

Chapter Four

Time

In a police statement concerning a criminal affair, absolute precision in matters of time and chronology is of the essence. A mistake of a few minutes in determining the exact moment of death of a murder victim can mean certain conviction, or freedom for the accused. Since Zola makes forensic and scientific claims for his novel, one expects that the question of time will be unproblematic and that *Thérèse Raquin* will unfold its events in strict succession. Nothing is further from the truth, and it can be difficult precisely to situate certain episodes in relationship to one another, although the reader of the novel has no difficulty in following the narrative. In every chapter Zola makes direct references to time, but such references are often vague and either concern events immediately preceding the moment in question or some imprecise continuity.

Written in 1866-67, towards the end of the Second Empire which will feature so powerfully in the *Rougon-Macquart, Thérèse Raquin* is not referentially rooted in contemporary history. The study of the criminal instincts of an adulterous couple is given as an exemplary case which will retain its validity for as long as men and women do not amend their ways. The opening chapter (describing the passage du Pont-Neuf in the present tense) is situated in a 'narratological present', with the indication that 'il y a quelques années' (66) a haberdasher's shop, *Thérèse Raquin,* used to be there. The description purports to be objective.

The second chapter is a flashback to the time when the Raquins lived in Vernon. Zola, before embarking on the story itself, gives his reader some background information about his characters; this technique is traditional and goes back to the oldest forms of known storytelling. Though no date within the nineteenth century is indicated, we are informed of the ages of his characters at the beginning of the story: Madame Raquin is over fifty, Camille twenty and Thérèse eighteen. A second flashback of sixteen years recalls Thérèse's arrival in Vernon. The timespan of the first chapter is therefore nineteen years, ending with Thérèse's marriage at twenty-one.

The opening of the third chapter, which marks the start of the action proper, is chronologically precise: 'huit jours après son mariage'(75), Camille expresses the wish to move to Paris. The following morning Madame Raquin announces that, the next day, she will travel to the capital and it would appear that she returns home the same evening. So far, so good. But then, within the next few pages of this chapter, we encounter the various devices used by Zola to anchor the narrative in time without adhering to a strict chronology:

a) Zola is *strictly precise:* ten days after the wedding, Madame Raquin goes to Paris;

b) he indicates that some times elapses, using an *imprecise expression:* 'au bout de quelques jours' her memory of the Passage du Pont-Neuf becomes rosier and rosier;

c) at a *precise* 'moment in time' indicated by 'enfin' (76), they leave for Paris, and this is followed by the *seemingly greater precision* of 'le soir du même jour' (77);

d) with *complete temporal vagueness* it is stated that 'Thérèse finit par s'impatienter' (77);

e) finally there is a return to *accuracy* mixed in with some*vagueness* concerning Camille's job hunt: 'Camille resta un mois sans trouver un emploi' (78).

Fictional time is elastic, and accelerates or slows down according to the narrative's internal needs or the relative emphasis the author wants to put on different episodes. The precipitation with which the decision to leave for Paris is taken betrays Camille's thoughtlessness and his mother's foolishness. It also serves to underline Thérèse's passivity. The exact time span that elapses between Madame Raquin's initial trip and the family's installation in the new 'home' is irrelevant and the indefinite adverb 'enfin' suffices to indicate their impatience. But if the date of the move is of little importance, the fact that it all takes place in one day needs to be emphasized, as it gives a measure of the shock that these three simple provincial people experience in landing in surroundings that are totally alien to them. Following this precipitation we get a gradual slowing down and even a temporary standstill: Thérèse, in a state of shock, refuses to cooperate and eventually prevents her aunt from tidying up the place.

This third chapter ends with the description of the boring, routine life led by the Raquins, the iterative imperfect tense giving the impression of a never-ending succession of eternally similar and petty actions. Finally, a temporal indication informs the reader that at the close of Chapter III three years have elapsed since the Raquins arrived in Paris.

The fourth chapter is another flashback, to an indeterminate rainy day when old Michaud took refuge in the passage and recognized Madame Raquin. The encounter goes back one or two years, since Michaud moved to Paris 'quelques mois' (80) after the Raquins. It would appear that the chance meeting took place on a Thursday, that impulsively Madame Raquin invited her friend that same evening, and so the tradition of the 'jeudis' was established. The scene is set for the crucial event that will plunge four very ordinary lives into a world of tragedy.

The meeting of Camille and Laurent is pure coincidence: it happens eighteen months after Laurent's entry into the same administration as Camille, on a Thursday evening. Again we have here a necessary temporal indication (a Thursday makes Laurent's invitation far more natural) lost in some vague continuity (we assume that the encounter occurs some three years after Camille's arrival in Paris). It is important, even without direct narratorial prompting, that the reader should bear in mind the time scale.

With Laurent's arrival, time accelerates. Camille's portrait is finished within days (a measure not of Laurent's genius but of his lack of commitment to painting), and Laurent's seduction of Thérèse is swiftly accomplished. The initial eight months of their affair are soon over and the narrative moves briskly, until that day when Laurent is prevented from running to their rendezvous. Chapter X marks a pause in the action, but is nonetheless crucial in Thérèse's and Laurent's relentless progression towards their criminal action. It reports the conversation in which Michaud holds forth about the failure of the police to catch all criminals. Coming some three weeks after Thérèse's visit to Laurent's garret, such chitchat spurs the lovers on, and the outing to Saint-Ouen seems to happen without delay. The impression is that these events follow one another in quick succession, especially since Zola does not put any extraneous episode in between. Yet there is a problem here. Laurent seduced Thérèse in summer (87); their affair runs smoothly for eight months (102); there follow a gap of two weeks before her visit to the Port aux Vins (103) and a further three weeks ('près de trois semaines' [110]) until Michaud spins his yarns of criminal impunity. In total this represents a little more than nine months: therefore the 'jeudi' in question takes place in *spring*. Yet the outing to Saint-Ouen was to be 'la dernière de la saison', since, with the coming of autumn, 'des souffles froids' are beginning to blow (114). Is Zola careless in his composition, or indifferent to the problems of chronology ?

Before attempting to answer this question, I should like to jump ahead, to Laurent's and Thérèse's wedding, when we encounter the same difficulties:

> Il y avait *près de deux ans* que les amants ne s'étaient trouvés enfermés dans la même chambre [...] depuis le jour où Thérèse était venue rue Saint-Victor. (173; my emphasis)

'Près de deux ans' since their last amorous encounter means late winter—early spring. But Michaud, the policeman, used almost an identical expression ('depuis bientôt deux ans' [160]) to measure the time passed since Camille's death until that evening when he first broached the subject of Thérèse's remarriage. One of the propositions is perforce erroneous unless one chooses to understand both expressions as meaning 'à peu près deux ans', i.e. a little more or less, a few months either side. The fact is that Zola had that option open to him and did not take it. Why? Is he careless or indifferent ? Perhaps a little careless. The chronology makes more or less sense, but is certainly elastic. The total duration of the action covers a span of almost exactly six years: Thérèse gets married soon after her twenty-first birthday, in spring. Her affair starts three years later: it is summer, she is twenty-four. Her *amours* are disrupted the following year, in late winter or early spring; Camille's murder takes place in the autumn: Thérèse is now twenty-five. Some fifteen months elapse, and she gets married to Laurent in December: she is twenty-six. Another few months, and the couple commit suicide in early summer: Thérèse is twenty-seven.

Six years is a long time, and I don't think that even the attentive reader closes the novel with the impression that so much time elapsed, especially not four years from the moment when Laurent meets Thérèse until their death. The lack of clarity has two causes:

a)   the tension between the perceived naturalistic obligation to explain events rationally (which requires the passing of time) and the dramatic necessity to concentrate the action in order to heighten the tragic impact;

b)   the importance of the meaning of the seasons. Springtime offers an ironic contrast to Thérèse's first, cold, marriage; her affair, on the other hand, appropriately starts in the summer, but the return of spring signals the disruption of the affair. Autumn lends a particular atmosphere to the murder, which would not have had the same overtones in summer. An irony of a different kind presides over the remarriage, staged in a cold and wet December. The contrast between the onlookers' perception of a happy union and the ghastly reality is underlined by the image of a blazing fireplace in winter which chars Thérèse and Laurent if they come too close to it, but does not warm their hearts or their bodies. Finally, the return of spring and of the first days of summer do not herald a new beginning. The easy-going outdoor life, so pleasant in the Parisian spring, is not for them.

In *Thérèse Raquin,* as in his other novels, Zola extends the perception of time by the use of flashback and flashforward. We have already mentioned the use of flashback in Chapter II, which charts, in broad sweeps, the characters' past life. A more subtle use of the technique occurs after Camille's death. As the body fails to appear for a whole week, the focus remains on Laurent, who every day, in a bluff and callous way, trots to the Morgue to check that morning's crop of corpses. Simultaneously, Madame Raquin and Thérèse retreat into themselves and suffer agony. For three days the shop remains closed. Rather than intermingle the two actions, Zola first describes Laurent's search and then, in a separate chapter covering the same period, the woman's descent into a tragic world.

The present extends into the past through the speech of the characters, for instance Laurent's accounts of his bohemian life or Thérèse's vilification of Camille in the comfort of her lover's arms. But, mostly, time extends forward with, in the first part, happy anticipation that will turn sour; and, in the second part, dreadful premonitions which fall short of the actual horror that will ensue. A few examples must suffice:

On the rare occasions when young Camille indulges in horseplay with a pubescent Thérèse, he feels no sexual stirrings ('sa chair n'avait pas un frémissement' [74]), whereas the girl wriggles with nervous laughter.

Returning from Paris, Madame Raquin declares: 'tu verras comme nous serons heureux dans ce coin-là', and adds: 'Va, nous ne nous ennuierons pas' (76). Commentary is quite superfluous here, but I should like to stress the conciseness of the false prediction. Madame Raquin and Thérèse will see their lives plunge into tragedy because of the move to Paris and because, precisely, the place where they are going to settle contains the essence of boredom and unhappiness.

Sitting at the card table, Thérèse has the feeling that she is locked up in a tomb, 'en compagnie de cadavres mécaniques' (82). Her death will occur at the very spot where she suffers from that hallucination just after the 'living dead', i.e. Michaud and company, have gone home at the end of another meaningless game of dominoes.

Attracted by the idea of becoming Thérèse's lover (and Madame Raquin's son), Laurent hesitates because things could go wrong. Trying to get too much, he could lose what he has already secured. He reflects on the risk of ending up in 'quelque mauvaise histoire' (90).

'Il tuait afin de vivre calme et heureux' (108). This is the ultimate irony, the criminal's delusion (we have already mentioned Macbeth), the hope that the crime will not be discovered and that no adverse consequences will follow.

The internal flashbacks or reminiscences, what Gérard Genette calls 'analepses internes' (*Figures III,* Paris, Seuil, 1972, pp. 90 ff.) proliferate in an hallucinatory manner after the murder and they are, obviously, concentrated on the figure of Camille, first as a ghost haunting his murderers, then as a living evocation conjured up by Thérèse to torment her second husband. No further examples are needed here, since the problem has already been discussed in connection with Camille's 'character'. What I should like to stress is the importance of the interweaving of the present with the past, and occasionally the future, on the part of the novelist, who thus brings out the lesson of the fable without having to preach or resort to didacticism. The telling feature is the contrast in the perception of the event by the characters and by the reader. The former, engaged as they are in the action and driven by their instinctual desires, are unable to foresee the consequences of their deeds. The latter, guided by Zola's rich patterning, is able to come to an informed judgement about the characters' behaviour.

Chapter Five

The Stage Adaptation

Zola had a passion for the theatre. According to his friend Alexis, he penned his first dramatic texts in his teens, while still at Aix. And four days before his death, on 25 September 1902, he wrote to Alfred Bruneau, the composer with whom he had collaborated on such works as *Messidor* ('drame lyrique', 1897) and *L'Ouragan* (1901), that his latest 'poème lyrique' in five acts, *Sylvanire ou Paris en amour* (not performed until 1924) was almost ready. Zola and Bruneau had begun their collaboration with the creation of *Le Rêve* ('drame lyrique en quatre actes', performed at the Paris Opéra-Comique, 18 June 1891) and together they revolutionized opera by introducing the prose libretto, peopled with 'des êtres vivants s'égayant de nos gaietés, souffrant de nos souffrances' (*O.C., XV, 529*). *Le Rêve* was a critical as well as a popular success. It was Zola's first in the theatre, and it is ironic that this champion of naturalism should have succeed in a genre which we do not associate with his name.

Professionally, Zola started his theatrical career as a critic in 1865. He was so prolific in his output that in June 1866 he could already publish a collection of essays in book form under the uncompromising title of *Mes haines*. His critical and journalistic activities continued unabated until 1881-2 (his main essays on theatre are published in *Le Naturalisme au théâtre* and *Nos auteurs dramatiques* [both 1881]).

Leaving *Thérèse Raquin* aside, Zola wrote five other plays for the theatre: *La Laide* (written 1865; first published in *O.C., XV*; never performed), *Madeleine* (written 1865; had a single, well-received performance at the Théâtre-Libre, 2 May 1889), *Les Héritiers Rabourdin* (1873-4; based on Ben Jonson's *Volpone,* premièred 3 November 1874; only 17 performances), *Le Bouton de rose* (1876-7; premièred in May 1878; 7 performances) and *Renée* (adapted from *La Curée,* 38 performances in April-May 1887). In addition, adaptations of his novels by Busnach were staged between 1879 and 1888 (e.g., *Nana* and *Germinal*), of which only the first, *L'Assommoir,* was a popular success, but at the price of cheapening and melodramatizing the novel. If the theorist was most influential, thanks to André Antoine's *mises en scène* at the Théâtre-Libre, Zola-the-playwright was singularly unsuccessful.

*****

The first performance of *Thérèse Raquin* took place in Paris on Friday 11 July 1873, at the Théâtre de la Renaissance. The director, Hippolyte Hostein, considered as a forerunner of Antoine's Théâtre-Libre, had courageously agreed to stage a play that many other more prestigious theatres had turned down. The *mise en scène* and the actors were generally praised; the play attracted more critical attention than any other production during that season, and the press was not as negative as many commentators have made out (Henri Mitterand includes a wide-ranging critical panorama in his edtion of the *Œuvres complètes*). The run of seventeen performances was, admittedly, short, but still respectable. The play was regularly revived until the start of the Second World War. The Théâtre de l'Odéon (the second national theatre of France) staged it with great success in 1905 and 1910. It was taken on a national tour in 1912 and, in 1920, it was put on in two different Parisian theatres. More recently, however, when directors were attracted by *Thérèse Raquin,* they tended to write their own adaptation of the novel rather than put on Zola's playtext. Marcel Carné's film of 1953 (with Simone Signoret and Raf Vallone in the major rôles) retains only the broad outlines of the novel: it is set in Lyon, and Vallone is an Italian lorry driver.

The Independent Theatre staged *Thérèse Raquin* in an English translation by A. Texeira de Mattos, directed by H. de Lange, at the Royalty Theatre, London, on 9 October 1891. It followed a controversial production of Ibsen's *Ghosts,* with which it was favourably compared. On the whole the critical reception was remarkably similar to that it received in Paris eighteen years earlier. The play was generally damned for having no literary merit, the set was condemned, but the actors applauded for creating memorable characters, although the Raquins were described as 'vulgar plebeians'. The critics objected to the 'terrible realism', though some were fascinated by its 'horror', for instance: 'a nightmare of horrors, a ghastly picture of human depravity and human weakness'. As in Paris, *Thérèse Raquin* was faulted by some critics for its undiluted romanticism, for its melodrama, while others deplored its insistence on naturalist details. At the other extreme, it could be judged to be too 'classic' for a naturalist play!

Thérèse Raquin, a concise synopsis

ACT I: One Thursday evening.

sc. i-iv: Supper is over, Laurent puts last touches to Camille's portrait.
v: 'Coup de théâtre'—Thérèse and Laurent are lovers, but meetings must end.
vi-xi: Arrival of *jeudistes*; hanging of portrait; trip to Saint-Ouen planned; silent compact between lovers.

ACT II: A year later. Another Thursday.

sc. i: The men and Mme Raquin play dominoes; Suzanne tells Thérèse about her romantic 'prince bleu'.
ii-vi: Thérèse's and Laurent's wedding is decided.

ACT III: A few weeks later. The wedding night. 3 a.m.

sc. i: Farcical interlude with Grivet and Michaud sticking nettles in bed.
ii: Mme Raquin and Suzanne prepare Thérèse for the night.
iii-v: The wedding night.
vi: Second 'coup de théâtre'—Mme Raquin overhears the truth about Camille's murder and collapses.

ACT IV: Some time later. Not a Thursday. 5 p.m.

sc. i: Suzanne will soon marry her 'prince bleu'. She tells of her visit to Laurent's studio.
ii-iii: Laurent returns from a long walk. The couple quarrel and express their fear of Mme Raquin.
iv-v: Grivet and Michaud pay an unexpected visit. Mme Raquin spells out her message: 'Thérèse et Laurent ont...' The *jeudistes* leave.
vi: Last quarrel. Thérèse and Laurent determined to kill each other.
Third 'coup de théâtre'—Mme Raquin stands up just as Laurent is about to kill her. She curses the murderers, who commit suicide.

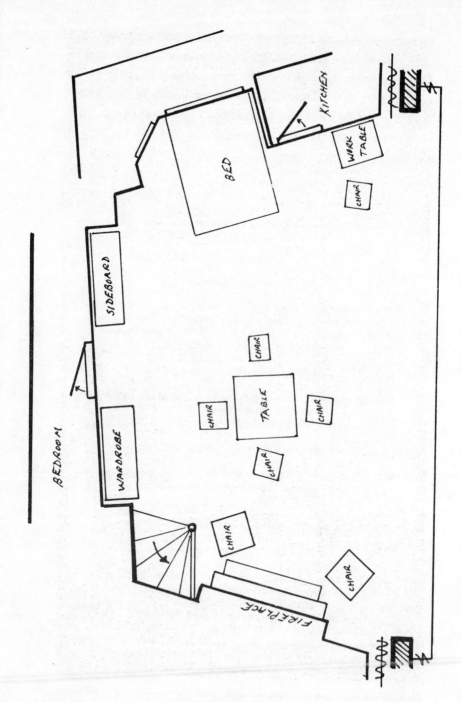

Thérèse Raquin: Plan

70

Design for *Thérèse Raquin*

71

Play Analysis

The set

For Zola, the environment in which the action of the play takes place is as important on the stage as it was in the novel, but the theatre critics tended to disagree. In his preface he sums up their objections: 'Fi de cette arrière-boutique! Fi de ces petites gens qui se permettent d'avoir un drame chez eux, à leur table couverte d'une toile cirée!' (*O.C.*, XV, 124). The critics objected to the fact that a tragedy was set in such common surroundings. Despite the innovations introduced by the Romantics, Musset and Hugo in particular, despite more and more frequent Shakespearian productions, the so-called 'séparation des genres' still exercised its tyranny and, as far as tragedy is concerned, it means that only people in high places, princes and princesses, are fit to figure in tragic tales; the corollary is that such tragic events must take place in palatial surroundings. The setting, deliberately ordinary, bordering on the sordid, shocked! But Zola, not satisfied with flying in the face of convention, 'foregrounds' his offending background by giving his characters plenty of trivial activities to perform, stage business not in keeping with the unfolding of a tragedy, thus destroying the idea, or ideal, of how a tragic character should behave.

The set plays a very important rôle, both naturalistically and symbolically, and one cannot stress enough the necessity of reading the stage directions most carefully: they matter as much as the dialogue.

The Raquins' room is a multi-purpose space: it combines Thérèse's bedroom, the dining-room and sitting-room, and has several entrances (the staircase to the shop, doors to the kitchen, to Madame Raquin's room and to the small corridor leading directly into the passage). Such an all-purpose location creates dramaturgical problems, but at first sight it conveys a feeling of chaos and indigence, which is the effect that Zola required. The place is 'noire', meaning dirty as well as black, 'délabrée' and badly in need of decoration ('tendue d'un papier gris déteint'). Artificial flowers and some photographs are the only derisory embellishment. A single window opens onto a 'mur nu', thereby increasing the feeling of oppression and imprisonment. The room is so cluttered with furniture that there is hardly any space for the characters to move. It contains a bed, a sideboard, a wardrobe, a worktable and a larger round table covered with an oilcloth, other unspecified pieces of furniture, two armchairs (one blue, one green), some chairs and boxes belonging to the haberdasher's trade. Such a set was so unusual, in 1873, that it was roundly condemned for its vulgarity, its 'réalisme impitoyable, révoltant' (*O.C.*, XV, 214).The 'unity of place' is respected, although Zola had originally planned a second act for the outing to Saint-Ouen.

In Madame Raquin's flat, nothing changes between Acts I and II: 'Une année s'est écoulée, sans rien changer à la chambre' (151). The only difference is that Camille's green armchair is empty. For Acts III and IV, the flat undergoes two dramatic and contradictory transformations, in which the naturalistic elements take on strong symbolic connotations. For the wedding, a splendid, virginal, yet sensuous décor has been generously and caringly prepared by Madame Raquin: 'La chambre est parée, toute blanche. Grand feu clair... Rideaux blancs au lit, couvre-pieds garni de dentelles... De gros bouquets de roses partout...' (169). To us, as to any open-minded spectator in 1873, Zola's intentions are obvious. We might be tempted to say 'too obvious', but we must not forget that such a 'thematic' use of stage setting, so profusely and imaginatively achieved in the contemporary theatre, was then innovatory. The same goes for the final appearance of the set: 'La chambre a repris son humidité noire. Rideaux sales. Ménage abandonné, poussière, torchons oubliés sur les sièges, vaisselle traînant sur les meubles. Un matelas roulé est jeté derrière un rideau du lit.' No words are needed to convey the extent of Thérèse's moral decline or the state of the marriage. The set tells its own story and provides a perfect visual and atmospheric commentary to her descent into an adulterous hell, with the harsh irony of a deceptive detour into marital bliss.

Stage business

At the time of *Thérèse Raquin*, playwrights and theatre directors were generally content with providing their plays with an elegant décor which actors did their utmost to ignore and to which spectators paid little attention.

Not only was Zola's set breaking with a time-honoured convention, but his *mise en scène* constantly drew attention to its physical presence. The characters' activities never allow the spectators to forget *where* the action takes place. Their trivial business increases the feeling of seediness and serves, on the one hand, to abolish the distance separating stage and auditorium and, on the other, to create the illusion of real life. Zola states in his preface: 'j'ai tenté de ramener continuellement la mise en scène aux occupations ordinaires de mes personnages, de façon à ce qu'ils ne "jouent" pas, mais à ce qu'ils "vivent" devant le public' (125).

From the moment the curtain opens, Zola's main concern is to create the impression that one is witnessing 'real' people living their everyday life, unaware of the presence of a viewer. The illusion of reality should be total. To create that illusion, Zola starts the play *in medias res*. The opening of the curtain does not signal the beginning of the action for the characters, it simply means that the spectator is now allowed to witness an action that started long before it became visible. And to emphasize the non-dramatic start, the spectator is invited to join the play at the precise moment when there is a lull in the action. The four characters have just finished their meal; an elderly woman is clearing the table while a younger woman sits, day-dreaming; of the two men, one is painting and the other is sitting. Zola's opening stage direction reads: 'Une grande paix, une grande douceur bourgeoise' (127).

Eventually the silence is broken by the sitter, who asks if he may speak. The ensuing conversation (during which we gradually learn the characters' names and are given clues to their relationships) captures perfectly that tired after-dinner mood when, as the French say, 'on parle pour ne rien dire'. The trivial subjects cover food, the past, Camille's health, the unhealthy flat, Laurent's 'artistic' and bohemian life, Thérèse's sulkiness... and one gets the impression that the same boring topics are endlessly rehearsed day after day. Nothing to announce an impending catastrophe. It is important, from a theatrical point of view, that the first act (with just one or two brief flashes of passion) be played as sedately as possible. The actors must forget that they act 'in a tragedy' and concentrate on living the passing moment. They are greatly helped in this by the naturalistic stage business suggested by the author (which they are invited to flesh out). During the first act the characters give the impression of being continually busy, even when they are off stage: Laurent, for instance, paints, tidies his brushes and tubes away, fetches a frame, fits the portait into the frame, hammers a picture hook into the wall and hangs the portrait, before sitting down to tea and a game of dominoes; Camille, after the sitting, changes into more comfortable clothes (with the help of his mother!), goes shopping returns with champagne and biscuits, drags his guests downstairs, organizes the seating arrangement; Madame Raquin, having tidied up the table and helped her son, fetches a lamp, prepares the little reception, welcomes the guests, picks up a lamp to show off the portrait, and disappears into the kitchen to return with the tea, which she pours out with the help of Suzanne; Thérèse absorbs herself in her embroidery; and even the two foolish guests fuss about obsessively with their umbrella, cane, galoshes or skullcap. Such activities are not gratuitous: they not only anchor the characters in a contemporary reality, but also serve to define their personality: Madame Raquin is dominant and hyperactive, Camille passive, Thérèse withdrawn, Michaud and Grivet ineffectual, Suzanne obliging, and Laurent is seemingly friendly and grateful.

The second act is less active. It starts at the precise point where the first act was interrupted: the *jeudistes* are playing dominoes and drinking tea, and the indomitable old lady, anxious not to waste a minute of her time, works at her knitting when not absorbed by the game. The third act, again, opens with a flurry of activity: returning from the wedding reception, Grivet and Michaud force their way into the nuptial chamber and stick nettles into the bed. Having chased them off, Madame Raquin and Suzanne prepare Thérèse for the night. Their conversation is punctuated by their naturalistic actions: undressing, combing, holding the night-gown to the fire, straightening the flowers. In this instance the stage business underlines the nervousness of the characters, and serves as a contrast to the harrowing scene between Thérèse and Laurent which is to follow.

It was the stage business of the fourth act which was most likely to give offence. In the first scene Thérèse and Suzanne chat, laugh, embroider, and knit as if they were without a care in the world. The mood changes quite swiftly with the imminent arrival of Laurent, but the murderess's activities do not grow in dignity: she lays the table, cleans a lettuce and, a little later, having just escaped retribution, she fetches soup, ladles it out and sits down to eat. Again the naturalistic details are not just there to fill in the picture, they are central to the main action. The final catastrophe is triggered by the fact that Thérèse forgot to give Laurent a spoon and because, according to him, she put too much salt into the soup. The suicides themselves are trivialized by the presence of the kitchen knife and the bottle of poison, clumsily dropped to the floor. The world of *Thérèse Raquin* is far removed from the worlds of Racine or Shakespeare and the murderers' deaths have nothing of the dignified, almost abstract quality of Phèdre's suicide or of the profoundly moving sacrificial deaths of Romeo and Juliet.

Zola *metteur en scène*

At the beginning of the Third Republic, the theatre director (*le metteur en scène*) as we know him today did not exist. Rehearsals were often haphazard and conducted by the theatre proprietor, the main actor in the company and/or the playwright; for instance, in *Nana,* the impresario Bordenave and the playwright Faucherry are directing operations at the Théâtre des Variétés, when Muffat intervenes to obtain the leading rôle in *La Petite Duchesse* for his mistress (*R.-M.,* II, 1321-31; 1337-46). As we have just seen, Zola took great care to write precise stage directions in order to help his actors to 'live' rather than 'perform' his play and he was particularly innovative in writing stage directions for *silent* moments. He recognized the importance of pauses in the dialogue, the impact of silent actions, the necessity to show that a character had a continuous organic life, like any human being, and not, as was too often the case, a kind of intermittent existence starting and stopping with every spoken line. Zola's most distinguished theatrical disciple, the *metteur en scène* André Antoine (1858-1943), founder of the Théâtre-Libre (1887-94), never tired of reminding his actors that the life of their characters carried on from one line to the next and even continued while off stage. In 1888, in his preface to *Miss Julie,* August Strindberg could still claim that he was renewing theatrical art by 're-introducing the art of the mime', by which he meant silent stage business. In *Thérèse Raquin* there are several speechless moments. We have already considered the silent opening scene, which helps to establish the right mood and atmosphere. The subsequent silent scenes all serve different purposes. Before Thérèse meets Laurent secretly, in Act I, sc. v, she is left on her own. In a 'jeu muet' Zola shows her transformation from being bored and tired into a woman who 'sourit, frémissante d'une joie subite' (134). To rush such a moment, in order 'to get on with the play', would be a great mistake, yet most nineteenth-century actresses would have skipped it without the peremptory indication of the author/director. This encounter, with the same gestures and the same words ('Toi, mon Laurent...') is repeated in Act III, sc. iv, after another silence, but robbed of the sensuality and the amorous expectation of the first. The contrast, before and after the murder, is rendered very poignantly by the parallelism of the presentation.

The repetition of the silent 'tea ceremony' at the end of Act I and the start of Act II provides a similar contrast. The trivial gestures and words to which no particular meaning is attached in the first instance become ominous and oppressive after Camille's murder, and it is indeed the very ordinariness of the situation in Act II which triggers Madame Raquin's despair. Seeing her friends assembled round the table she bursts into tears: 'Je ne puis pas, je ne puis pas... Quand je vous vois tous comme autrefois, autour de cette table, je me souviens, mon cœur se fend...' (152) . Her own world has collapsed around her, yet nothing has changed!

Another kind of 'silent acting' is inscribed in some scenes in which two separate actions take place simultaneously. A couple of examples will suffice. The two young women never play dominoes, and during the game of Act II, sc. i, Suzanne tells Thérèse about her fairy-tale 'prince bleu', a charming young man met at the Jardin du Luxembourg. The action is therefore divided between Suzanne's half-whispered, but excited storytelling and the animation round the domino table. The second example of simultaneity occurs in Act IV, sc. v, as Madame Raquin tries to spell out her message. The *jeudistes* play out a black comedy, while the murderers sink deeper and deeper into their tragedy. As well as keeping the two strands going side by side, it is imperative that the actors playing Grivet, Michaud and—particularly—Suzanne be not affected by the tension and the intensity of their fellow-actors: comedy and tragedy must follow their separate ways.

Such remarks might appear superfluous to modern theatregoers used to a thorough 'naturalistic' style of acting. Even if unaware of the theories of Antoine, Stanislavski or Lee Strasberg, every modern spectator has ample experience of total illusionistic acting in television and cinema. But Zola, the champion of naturalism, had to fight on several fronts. It was not enough to write a new style of plays, he had also to ensure that he found capable and willing interpreters.

Dialogue and Dramatic Irony

'Les romanciers naturalistes ont déjà écrit d'excellents modèles de dialogues ainsi réduits aux paroles strictement nécessaires' (*NT*, 172). Such an assertion immediately prompts a question: what is meant by 'strictly necessary speeches'? In the first scene, for instance, is it necessary:

a)   that Camille should tell Laurent that he (Laurent) likes custard?

b)   that Mme Raquin should mention that Thérèse added icing sugar?

c)   that Laurent should reminisce about apples bought by Camille, and Camille about knives bought by Laurent when they were boys in Vernon?

d)   for Camille to inform Laurent of a chilly draught coming through the small side door?

e)   for Mme Raquin to remind Camille that she offered to return to Vernon?

f)   and for Camille to riposte that he will not return, 'maintenant que j'ai retrouvé Laurent à l'administration' (129) ?

The style of the dialogue in which these statements are made is simple and straightforward; the sentences are short and contain few clauses; the vocabulary is easy to understand. Four people at the end of a meal could indeed speak these lines. But their dialogue would not, as a rule, be as structured and as dense as it is here. In this opening scene, every little trivial piece of information has a meaning beyond its immediate, literal significance and contributes to the rich pattern of dramatic irony that Zola weaves throughout the play. Beyond the literal meaning, then, the 'subtext' of the points mentioned tells us that:

a) Meals are cooked to please Laurent; he usurps the place of the favourite son;

b) Thérèse's unexpected and out-of-character intervention contradicts her hostility (and looks ironically forward to the last scene when she puts too much salt into the soup!);

c) Camille's purchases were harmless, and the apples shared between the 'boys'; Laurent's fascination with knives betrays the violence of his character;

d) It is through the hostile corridor that Camille's misfortune makes its entrance (added irony: the line is spoken to Laurent);

e) Mme Raquin offers her son a chance to escape his tragic fate;

f) But he refuses, mistaking evil for good.

Zola could not expect his spectators to appreciate the intricacies of his deceptively simple dialogue on first hearing it in the theatre, nor is it necessary in order to understand and enjoy the drama. But as the patterning continues throughout the play, the spectator is gradually alerted to this internal dramatic irony. The most obvious examples of irony concern Madame Raquin. In Act II, sc. v and vi, for instance, she believes that she has finally convinced Thérèse to marry Laurent and she says through her tears: 'Ce sera mon dernier printemps... Laurent nous aimera bien... Tu sais que je l'épouse un peu, moi aussi. Tu me le prêteras pour mes petites commissions...'(166). It will be her last spring indeed, but not as she fondly imagines it. And she speaks the ultimate ironic line at the end of the second act: 'Vous me donnez bien de la joie. Je demanderai au ciel qu'il ne nous punisse pas' (168).

Being the adaptation of a novel, the play, unfortunately, contains too many instances when a character does not so much address his partner, as impart information to the spectator. During the furtive and dangerous encounter between the lovers in Act I, sc. v, Thérèse is given a long speech recalling her life, from childhood to marriage! And at the very end, the crescendo towards the climax of the tragedy is interrupted by the account of the murder, which Zola had not mentioned before. There are also several instances of asides, which are not integrated into the naturalistic fabric of the play, but to which Zola resorts in order to inform the spectator of the moods or inner reactions of his characters. Thérèse's last aside, for instance, is unnecessary melodramatic. Hiding the knife, she murmurs: 'Jamais je n'aurai la patience d'attendre la nuit. Le couteau me brûle la main' (201).

The speech pattern remains virtually the same throughout the play, despite Zola's statement that 'chaque causeur' should have a 'tour d'esprit particulier' (*NT*, 171). In such an emotionally charged drama as *Thérèse Raquin*, one would expect an idiomatic and at times an idiosyncratic turn of phrase, yet there is never any lapse in the very precise syntax spoken by all characters. Taunting Laurent, daring him to drink the poison, Thérèse does not forget to use the highly correct, but literary, imperfect subjunctive: 'Camille était bon, entends-tu, et je voudrais que *tu fusses* à sa place dans la terre' (199).

Judging from the dialogue in his novels, especially in *L'Assommoir*, is it fair to conclude that the novelist was a better playwright than the dramatist? Or rather, that the novelist had the courage to follow his own inspiration, whereas the dramatist, despite the theorist's bold assertions, was afraid to go too far?

From novel to stage

Zola was determined to put a 'slice of life' on the stage. Rather than write an original play, he decided to adapt an existing novel. In his preface, he explains, disingenuously, that he turned *Thérèse Raquin* into a play because some critics 'm'avaient formellement mis au défi d'en tirer un drame'(121). More positively, he affirms that he had found in his novel a 'milieu' and 'des personnages' which would allow him to carry out his experiment. He repeats that his aims are to achieve 'une analyse exacte' and to help the theatre in its attempts at realizing an art made of 'vérité et science expérimentale'. These aims were largely reached in the physical presentation of the play (set, props, stage business, characterization). But it must also be said that, from novel to stage, many powerful and essential ingredients got lost.

Zola rightly states that the strength of *Thérèse Raquin* lies in 'les combats intérieurs des personnages'(123) rather than in the anecdote. Unfortunately these interior battles are better suited to the novel, where each character's state of mind, his every change of mood, his hopes and fears can be subtly analysed. The theatre, at least until Beckett's *Krapp's Last Tape* or *Not I*, was not the medium for analytical introspection. For instance, in the novel, Zola writes that during the wedding night Thérèse and Laurent 'causèrent de la pluie et du beau temps' in order to keep the ghost at bay, and he illustrates his point with a few platitudes rendered in reported speech. The message is clear for the reader, who conjures up in his mind a perfect picture of the tormented murderers. On the stage, however, the actors speak the lines and what they have to say is:

> Thérèse.   ...les abricotiers feront bien de ne pas se presser de fleurir.
>
> Laurent.   Les coups de gelée, en mars, sont très mauvais pour les arbres fruitiers. (176)

Such a contrived dialogue breaks the *effet de réel*. Although the lines are perfectly ordinary, they have an absurd ring about them and if they were inserted into the dialogue of *La Cantatrice chauve* no one, not even Ionesco himself, would find them out of place. A situation which, in the novel, is gripping here borders on the ridiculous. One can only subscribe to the judgement of the most enlightened critic of the first night who put his finger on the central problem: 'Le sujet même, si profondément dramatique, est anti-théâtral' (216).

We cannot list, let alone analyse, all that was lost from novel to play. I shall concentrate on the more 'dramatic' examples, by which I mean particularly powerful elements in their physical manifestations which, at first sight, would translate marvellously to the stage and yet either got lost or were weakened by the transfer. The theatre is the art of physical presence par excellence, yet paradoxically it is the physically most successful episodes of the novel that suffered most. Sex and violence are notoriously difficult to stage. What can be described in detail in the novel, or shown with a greater or lesser degree of taste on the screen, can soon become tasteless, repulsive or pornographic on the stage. Conversely, scenes like Laurent's attacks on Thérèse run the risk of becoming titillating when they should inspire fear. Consequently the sado-masochistic relationship between the lovers is reduced to a hug in Act I, sc. v ('Laurent la prend dans ses bras' [135]), and to threatening attitudinizing in Act IV, sc. vi ('Il la jette à genoux devant la table et lève le poing' [200]). François, the cat, was an inevitable casualty—although he made a startling comeback in the BBC television adaptation. The absence of the bite on Laurent's neck is more puzzling. It cannot be simply explained by the problem of making it visible from the stage. Its suppression is regrettable because it robs the play of a symbolic dimension, and the actor of interesting and revealing movements and postures. Also downgraded is the importance of the portrait; Thérèse's whoring as well as her pregnancy are cut; and such changes soften the impact of the play. As a final example, consider the 'mobility' of the paralysed Madame Raquin. In the novel she is carried from bed to dining-room in Laurent's arms and the unnatural intimacy of the geature between two people who harbour murderous thoughts for each other is as *theatrical* as it is dramatic. In the play, wheels are fitted to the armchair and the invalid is simply pushed in and out, thus robbing Madame Raquin's single entrance as a paralytic of much of its drama. Why substitute a highly effective theatrical action with some meaningless stage business, when the former can be more economically achieved than the latter? My guess is that Zola was afraid that his audience would not have stood for it and that it would have been considered 'obscene'. It is also likely that a 'respectable' actress would herself have balked at the suggestion.

Zola was right to have misgivings about a stage adaptation of *Thérèse Raquin*. Even if, in terms of 'theatrical naturalism', the production of the play achieved much that is to be applauded, its relative success cannot be compared to the success of the novel.

Chapter Six

Thérèse Raquin and the Poetics of Naturalism

In the Novel

As stated in the preface to the second edition, in *Thérèse Raquin,* Zola aimed at studying 'des tempéraments et non des caractères' (59). His characters, he claims, are driven by their body ('leurs nerfs et leur sang'), he denies them any free will and he posits that Thérèse and Laurent are 'des brutes humaines' devoid of souls: 'l'âme est parfaitement absente, j'en conviens aisément, puisque je l'ai voulu ainsi' (60). In contrast to the 'psychological' bias, as Zola would have it, of the literature of the past, he is determined to stress the importance of the 'physiological'. In this preface, the theorist and controversialist is carried away by his own enthusiasm and he looks over the shoulder of the novelist during the entire narrative, intervening at regular intervals to make sure that the theoretical drift does not get lost because of the interest created by the exceptional events recounted in the novel. This is not a place to enter into a philosophical or theological debate about the existence of the soul, and its nature if it exists. Nor can we open a debate on morals and morality. I shall assume that the two problems are linked, that the 'existence' of the soul and of a moral sense is what sets humanity apart and, if this is so, Thérèse and Laurent are human and possess in themselves a clear notion of the difference between right and wrong. Zola the theorist had the ambition to write an 'étude physiologique' (62) making scientific claims, but Zola the novelist with his deeper intuitive understanding wrote a text replete with poetic connotations, which the theorist constantly felt the need to redirect. We have, therefore, a novel on two levels, two strains of writing in contradiction with each other.

The murder of Camille instantaneously plunges Thérèse into a horrific nether world of nightmares, and every passing day renders her torture more unbearable. Laurent is allowed a little respite, but when hallucinations take hold of him, he is just as firmly trapped in his guilt. Guilt ? Zola studiously avoids any discussion of guilt. The epithet 'coupable' is never used for the murderers of Camille and occurs only twice in Michaud's and Grivet's ludicrous conversation about police inefficiency. Of guilt, as such, there is never any mention, although, as we have remarked, Zola-the-moralist tends to intervene from time to time in the narrative to pass comment, as when he writes about Thérèse, during the heady days of her passion, that 'elle savait qu'elle faisait le mal' (100). But he would have argued that knowledge of one's own evil-doing did not imply a feeling of guilt!

The nub of the naturalist/physiological thesis is presented in Chapter XXII, which, following the wedding night, is largely analytical before plunging more deeply into the present reality of the murderers. Zola takes stock of the situation and explains how and why the former lovers, now free to enjoy each other's company, are... Are what, in fact ? Racked by guilt and remorse? It would appear so. Not so, says Zola. Guilt and remorse are psychological notions: Laurent and Thérèse are immune to such emotions. Their contradictory physical natures have acted on each other and both have been perverted. The effects are most noticeable in the case of Laurent, who is now prey to an 'effroi éternel' (183). But we should not jump to the wrong, psychological, conclusion: 'ses remords étaient purement physiques'! What *physical* remorse is I do not know, and Zola does not explain. Or, rather, he paints that remorse most hauntingly, but Laurent's conscience is not affected, so much so that he would commit the crime again, if he thought that it would serve his interests. Such an affirmation is inconsistent: a reasonably intelligent person would not freely repeat a mistake, knowing the consequences. The most extreme statement of the physiological thesis reads: 'Le corps souffrait horriblement, l'âme restait absente' (184). Here Zola would appear to be postulating an absolute separation between body and soul, but earlier he presented a more subtle reading of the situation, linking the two together and affirming an interpenetration of the physiological and psychological (see 154). At other points, he hints vaguely at feelings that the murderers experience, which the novelist cannot properly apprehend: 'il se fit en eux un travail sourd' (140) and 'il est difficile à l'analyse de pénétrer à de telles profondeurs' (203). Such analysis is the stuff of the novel: it is there, page after page, and denials cannot hide from the reader the painstaking painting of remorse leading to suicide. On one occasion at least, without any ambiguity, Zola postulates this in Thérèse:

> Parfois, Thérèse était prise de remords, en face de ce masque blafard sur lequel coulaient silencieusement de grosses larmes. Elle montrait sa tante à Laurent, le conjurait du regard de se taire. (221)

Already, before their marriage, the murderers felt 'l'impérieuse nécessité de s'aveugler' (157). To blind oneself to an unbearable reality in order to escape into a world of make-believe is, in this instance, an effort to repress feelings of guilt and remorse so strong that life would become unlivable if such feelings were allowed to well up to the surface.

Their suicide is caused, precisely, because they are overwhelmed by guilt. In my opinion, Thérèse and Laurent, especially Thérèse, are presented as highly moral characters who by the circumstances of their lives have been driven to murder. They would, it goes without saying, be more moral if they did not succumb—but than we would have no novel. Given the crime, then, they never forgive themselves or each other. Where French justice might have been lenient for a crime of passion carried out on impulse, they condemn themselves to death. Looking into each other's eyes, they confess their guilt: 'Ils lisaient des aveux dans leurs yeux' (225). And the last look they exchange is one of thanks: 'Ils échangèrent un dernier regard, un regard de remerciement' (253).

'Des brutes humaines, rien de plus', states Zola (60). Thérèse is driven by her evil instinct, her evil femininity, and Laurent is a thick-skinned animal impervious to any emotion, acting only to satisfy his grossest physical needs. In order to persuade his readers to see Laurent in that wholly negative light, Zola strews his text with remarks about his lack of conscience and awareness of the consequences of his action. Zola's determination to paint him as a 'brute humaine' is most clearly apparent in the Parisian scenes immediately following the murder. First, while Michaud breaks the news of Camille's drowning to Madame Raquin, Laurent walks into a pâtisserie and stuffs himself full of cakes, glancing at the passing girls. Later that evening, when Thérèse has been put to bed, he 'strolls' back home with a feeling of satisfaction: 'La fraîcheur le pénétrait de bien-être; [...] Il flânait' (128).

Throughout the novel, Zola stresses the pre-eminence of physical impulses. Blind sexual drives bring Thérèse and Laurent together. Only their bodies suffer when their liaison must cease (111), only their bodies crave for a reunion ('son organisme réclamait les caresses violentes de Laurent...' [157]). Being only bodies, it is therefore not surprising that the body takes over the moral control of the entire personality. As we have seen, the wound caused by Camille's bite does not heal: the 'moral' canker is expressed in purely physical terms. It is no less an expression of remorse for all that. In the preface, the fact that the murderers' bodies recoil from one another is described as 'une rébellion du système nerveux tendu à se rompre' (60). Where, on the dissecting table, in which sinews, limbs or blood globules, does the physician find the source of such a revolt ? If such evidence can be traced into the physiological make-up of two human mammals, the same evidence could be brought to light in the autopsy of a wild animal that has just killed a dominant male in order to take over his reproductive prerogative. Such a proposition is patently absurd. In the animal world, Laurent's action, far from being a crime, would be encouraged, for it ensures the survival of the fittest and a steady improvement of the genetic stock.

In *Le Roman expérimental* (1879), Zola is still using a physiological/ medical vocabulary to define the work of the naturalist novelist, but he also accepts the moral dimension in the discussion of human behaviour: 'Nous sommes [...] des moralistes expérimentateurs, montrant par l'expérience de quelle façon se comporte une passion dans un milieu social' (*RE*, 76). Again and again, he compares the art of the novelist to the work of a 'moraliste expérimentateur', whose task it is to help humanity to master the powers of good and evil, to regulate society and to help the action of justice by exploring the ways criminals operate. These aims, although expressed in a stubbornly polemical fashion in the Preface, are already those pursued by the author of *Thérèse Raquin,* and the novel remains one of his most hauntingly evocative, a harrowing study of the destructive effects on human minds of obsessional remorse and obsessive desire for revenge.

On Stage

> En un mot, le théâtre est le domaine de la convention; tout y est conventionnel, depuis les décors, depuis la rampe qui éclaire les acteurs par en bas, jusqu'aux personnages qu'on y promène au bout d'un fil. La vérité ne saurait y entrer qu'en petites doses distribuées adroitement. On va même jusqu'à jurer que le théâtre n'aurait plus sa raison d'être, le jour où il cesserait d'être un amusant mensonge. (*NT*, 164)

As a critic, Zola never ceased to thunder against the theatre of his time and against its outmoded conventions, of which it had to rid itself in order to be renewed. How could a renewal come about? 'Il s'agira simplement', answers Zola, 'de changer la facture, la carcasse de l'œuvre' (*NT*, 169). *Simplement* is soon said! How, indeed, does one transform a seemingly eternal formula of play construction ('la facture'), a traditional dramatic framework ('la carcasse')? 'Simply', says Zola, by importing into the new dramaturgy some of the ingredients which have made the nineteenth-century novel so successful. And he boldly affirms that the best kind of theatre is to be found in the novels of Balzac. If this is so, why is Balzac a failed playwright? Because a play is not a novel, and Zola was well aware of the difference since he opens the preface to his adaptation by stating categorically: 'J'estime qu'il est toujours dangereux de tirer un drame d'un roman.' (*O.C.*, XV, 121)

The naturalistic novel relies heavily on detailed character presentation and analysis, on minute psychological studies, on careful investigations of the interaction between individuals, between people and their environment, on searching analyses of interpersonal relationships, on rich and sometimes lengthy descriptions... All these elements, somehow or other, Zola would like to see introduced in the drama. As far as he is concerned, to show 'la double influence des personnages sur les faits et des faits sur les personnages' (*NT*, 169) is as paramount in the theatre as it is in the novel. 'Le roman analyse longuement, avec une minutie de détails où rien n'est oublié; le théâtre analysera *aussi brièvement qu'il le voudra* par les actions et les paroles.' (*ibid.*; my emphasis)

Zola calls for the 'novelization of the theatre' ('la romanisation du théâtre'). That is to say that a play, like a novel, should know no boundaries and present a multiplicity of points of view, of locations, of characters, of props... It should enjoy an unfettered timespan and be allowed to move in any direction. In short, like the novel, theatre should have an open structure. In his theoretical writings Zola often praises the neo-classical French playwrights, and he openly admires Molière and Racine. But just as often he dismisses the sacrosanct unities of time and place, claiming for the playwright total freedom of creation. What he is dreaming of is what we today call 'epic theatre', the theatre that Brecht and Piscator conceived, wrote and staged in Germany during the inter-war years and that has come to influence theatre writing and theatre practice the world over. No one in France at the end of the nineteenth-century came anywhere near the conception of that modern theatre, and Zola-the-dramatist never attempted to put the ideas of Zola-the-theorist into practice.

The main reason, as I see it, for Zola's failure to put his own dramatic precepts to the test was his uncompromising insistence on the pre-eminence of the set. The theatre, he affirms, is 'une évocation matérielle de la vie' and he asks rhetorically: 'La décoration n'est-elle pas une description continue, qui peut être beaucoup plus exacte et saisissante que la description faite dans un roman?' (NT, 170) He concludes emphatically that sets and properties are always necessary components of a theatrical performance and that a precise replica of reality is 'une condition essentielle d'existence [du théâtre]' (NT, 171). I have briefly alluded to Zola's magnificent, and often hallucinatory, descriptions in the Rougon-Macquart: not a single page of these novels could be rendered in a more 'exacte et saisissante' manner on the stage than it is in the book. The shock value of certain episodes, like the notorious cat-fight in the lavoir of L'Assommoir, is greater on the stage because of its immediacy and because of the public nature of the event, but this is not the issue. The stimulation of the spectator's imagination in the theatre is of a completely different order to the stimulation of the imagination of the solitary reader, free to procede at leisure and engaging in a silent but creative dialogue with the author.

Practically and aesthetically, the contradictions in Zola's aspirations to be free from all conventions and his insistence on building illusionistic three-dimensional set are insuperable. Practically, it is impossible to shift one heavy set after another without causing delays detrimental to the dramatic rhythm of the play. Aesthetically, even if it were technically feasible, the appearance and disappearance, in quick succession, of fully-constructed sets, precise in every detail and replete with 'naturalist' objects, would submerge the actors, drown the dialogue and stifle the spectator's response. It would also negate the illusion of reality, which is the aim pursued by the naturalist playwright.

The Swedish dramatist August Strindberg so admired Zola that he translated his naturalist tragedy, *The Father,* into French himself in order to get the opinion of *le Maître.* He also put forward a comprehensive résumé of Zola's ideas on theatre in his preface to *Miss Julie.* Both these masterpieces adhere to the unities of time and place, of tone and action, and Zola's conceptual influence can be detected. But Strindberg moved on, leaving outmoded nineteenth-century concepts behind him and laying the foundations of the theatre of the twentieth-century with plays like *To Damascus* and *A Dream Play.* In these plays Strindberg did put Zola's revolutionary ideas into practice (although it would be wrong to postulate a direct influence of Zola on Strindberg at that point in his career), creating a dramatic structure and a dramatic movement as free of conventions as the novel. As the title of *A Dream Play* implies, the new dramaturgy has also moved beyond 'materialist naturalism' and is now ready to incorporate the life of the spirit and the irrational. Such a move is paralleled in Zola's lyrical works written in the last ten years of his life and in his final prose works *Les Trois Villes* and *Les Quatre Evangiles.* Unfortunately, as a dramatist, Zola lacked the radical streak which made him such an influential critic and such a masterful novelist.

Conclusion

The 1990 Herbert Read Memorial Lecture (ICA, London, and BBC 2, 6 February) brought together two successful writers: the novelist Salman Rushdie, author of *The Satanic Verses,* and the dramatist Harold Pinter. Rushdie, still forced to live in hiding because of the threats against his life, asked Pinter to deliver his text, entitled 'Is Nothing Sacred?' Zola never had to go into hiding, although he had to flee to England in 1898 at the height of the Dreyfus Affair. The controversy surrounding the publication of *The Satanic Verses* helps to remind us of the power of literature and of the passions that works of fiction can arouse. In France, many of Zola's novels attracted storms of protest. In England, some of his novels were banned for a time, and his English publisher, Ernest Vizetelly, was jailed for three months, in May 1889, for having published 'obscene' material.

Rushdie asserts that 'literature, by asking extraordinary questions, opens new doors in our minds'. Zola, starting with *Thérèse Raquin*, never tired of asking extraordinarily uncomfortable questions: about heredity and human sexuality, about working and living conditions in the slums of Paris or in mining villages, about financial and political power, about corruption. The list is endless: he painted the ravages of alcoholism and the underworld of prostitution; he grappled with the problems of bigotry, of religious fanaticism... Despite his claims to be an exact scientist, Zola was working at the frontiers of knowledge as far as human behaviour is concerned.

Rushdie further affirms that 'the novel is best suited to challenge absolutes of all kinds' and that, since the novelist only needs pen and paper, the novel is the art form that is 'least compromised' and in which the artist enjoys the greatest freedom of expression. Conversely, the conventions pertaining to theatre may account for Zola's lack of success on the stage.

The novelist, concludes Rushdie, is the artist who constantly re-imagines, re-thinks and re-invents the world. Zola would have enthusiastically subscribed to the formula, he who for forty years re-imagined, re-thought and re-invented the world we live in.

Suggestions for Further Reading

The complete works of Zola, the fifteen-volume *Œuvres complètes* (*O.C.*), are edited by Henri Mitterand (Paris: Tchou, "Cercle du Livre Précieux", 1966-1970).

Les Rougon-Macquart (*R.-M.*), in five volumes, are edited by Henri Mitterand (Paris: N.R.F. Gallimard, coll."Bibliothèque de la Pléiade", 1960-1967).

Zola's early correspondence is contained in *Correspondance,* I, 1858-1867 (*Corr.*), edited by B.H. Bakker (Paris: C.N.R.S / Montréal: Presses de l'Université, 1978).

On Zola and *Thérèse Raquin*

Armstrong, Judith	*The Novel of Adultery*. London, Macmillan, 1976.
Bertrand-Jennings, Chantal	*Espaces romanesques: Zola.* Sherbrooke, Québec, Naaman, 1987.
_____	*L'Eros et la femme chez Zola*. Paris, Klincksieck, 1977.
_____	'Zola féministe?', *Les Cahiers naturalistes,* 44 (1972), 172-87 and 45 (1973), 1-22.
Best, Janice	*Expérimentation et adaptation: essai sur la méthode naturaliste d'Emile Zola,* Paris, José Corti, 1986, pp. 43-58.
Carter, Lawson A.	*Zola and the Theater*. Paris, P.U.F. / New Haven, Conn.,Yale University Press, 1963.
Claverie, Michel	*'Thérèse Raquin* ou les Atrides dans la boutique du Pont-Neuf', *Les Cahiers naturalistes,* 36 (1968), 138-47.
Dugan, Raymond	'La psychologie criminelle dans *Thérèse Raquin',* *Travaux de linguistique et de littérature,* Strasbourg, XVII, 2, (1979), 131-7.

Foucard, Claude	'La partie de campagne', *Missions et démarches de la critique,* Paris, Klincksieck, 1973, pp. 795-805.
Furst, Lilian R.	'A Question of Choice in the Naturalist Novel', *Proceedings of the Comparative Literature Symposium,* V (1972), 39-53.
————	'Zola's *Thérèse Raquin*: A Re-evaluation', *Mosaic,* V, 3 (Spring 1972), 189-202.
Gahide, Françoise	'Le naturalisme au théâtre', *Théâtre populaire,* 31 (September 1960), 1-11.
Hemmings, F.W.J.	*Emile Zola.* Oxford, Clarendon Press, (2nd edition), 1966.
————	'The Origins of the Terms *naturalisme, naturaliste',* French Studies, VIII (1954), 109-121.
Jennings, Chantal	'*Thérèse Raquin* ou le péché originel', *Littérature,* 23 (1978), 94-101.
Kaempfer, Jean	*Emile Zola, d'un naturalisme pervers.* Paris, José Corti, 1989.
Lapp, John C.	'The Watcher Betrayed and the Fatal Woman: Some Recurring Patterns in Zola', *P.M.L.A.,* 74 (1959), 276-84.
de Lattre, Alain	*Le Réalisme selon Zola: archéologie d'une intelligence.* Paris, P.U.F, 1975.
Lethbridge, Robert	'Zola, Manet and *Thérèse Raquin', French Studies,* 34 (1980), 278-99.
Mitterand, Henri	*Zola et le naturalisme.* Paris, P.U.F,'Que sais-je?', no. 2314, 1986.
————	*Le Discours du roman.* Paris, P.U.F, 1980.
Rickert, Blandine	'*Thérèse Raquin:* observations sur la structure dramatique du roman', *Les Cahiers naturalistes,* 55 (1981), 42-51.
Ripoll, Roger	'Fascination et fatalité: le regard dans l'œuvre de Zola', *Les Cahiers naturalistes,* 32 (1966), 104-116.